NEGATIVE DOUBLES

By Marty Bergen

Bergen Books

Bergen Books
9 River Chase Terrace
Palm Beach Gardens, FL 33418-6817

First Edition published 2000.
Printed in the United States of America.
10 9 8 7 6 5 4 3 2

First Printing: July, 2000
Second Printing: April, 2008

Library of Congress Control Number: 2008901120

ISBN: 0-9744714-5-3

Dedication

To Luella Slaner

My student, my partner, but most of all, my friend.

Table of Contents

Foreplay 1

Overview 3

The Quintessential Convention 5
    Comparing Negative and Takeout Doubles   5
    Points Needed for a Negative Double   6
    What's the Point?   7
    How High?   9
    Non-Negative Doubles   11

Unbid Suits 12
    Four Spades or Five?   12
    1 Minor - (1 or 2 of Major)   14
    1 Minor - (2 Other Minor)   15
    1 Major - (1 or 2 of Other Major)   16
    Suits Promised by a Negative Double   17
    Responder Makes a Jump Shift in Competition   18

Opener's Rebids 20
    Bid Your Three-Card Major Under Duress   20
    Opener Rebids a Five-Card Suit   22
    Opener's Strong Bids   23
    Opener Rebids Notrump   24
    Reopening Doubles   25
    The Penalty Pass   27

Stop—Read This 29

Negative Doubles at the One Level 30
    1♣ - (1♢) - Dbl   30
    1 Minor - (1♡) - Dbl   32
    1 Minor- (1♠) - Dbl   34
    1♡ - (1♠) - Dbl   36
    A Negative Double with a Six-Card Suit   38

Negative Doubles at the Two Level 39
    1♢ - (2♣) - Dbl   40
    1 Major - (2♣) - Dbl   42
    1♣ - (2♢) - Dbl   44
    1 Major - (2♢) - Dbl   46
    1 Minor - (2♡) - Dbl   48
    1♠ - (2♡) - Dbl   50
    1 Minor - (2♠) - Dbl   52
    1♡ - (2♠) - Dbl   54

Negative Doubles at the Three Level 57
    1♣ - (3♣) - Dbl   58
    1♢ - (3♣) - Dbl   60
    1 Major - (3♣) - Dbl   62
    Thrump Doubles   64
    1♣ - (3♢) - Dbl   66
    1♢ - (3♢) - Dbl   68
    1 Major - (3♢) - Dbl   70
    1 Minor - (3♡) - Dbl   72
    1♠ - (3♡) - Dbl   74
    1 Minor - (3♠) - Dbl   76
    1♡ - (3♠) - Dbl   78

Negative Doubles at Higher Levels 80
    Negative Doubles at the Four Level   80
    Opener's Unique 4♦ Bid   81
    1♦ - (4♣) - Dbl   82
    1 Major - (4♣) - Dbl   84
    1♣ - (4♦) - Dbl   86
    1 Major - (4♦) - Dbl   88
    4NT Takeout after a Four of a Major Overcall   90
    1 Minor - (4♥) - Dbl   92
    1♠ - (4♥) - Dbl   94
    1 Minor - (4♠) - Dbl   96
    1♥ - (4♠) - Dbl   98
    1 Suit - (5 Minor) - Dbl   100
    Preserving all Options   102

Advanced Treatments 103
    Responder's Three-Card Suits   103
    Responder's Jump Cuebid as a Transfer to 3NT   104
    One Time Only —You Can "Preempt a Preempt"   106

Alternative Lifestyle 107
    Four-Four or Four-Three?   107
    1 Minor - (1♥) - 1♠ with Just Four?   108
    Thrump 3♠   109
    Low-Level Negative Doubles with No Unbid Major   110

Partnership Checklists 112
    Bread and Butter Issues   112
    Opener's Bread and Butter Issues   113
    Advanced Issues   114

Bridge Jargon 115

Learning With Marty 116

Bridge Books by Marty Bergen

Bergen for the Defense

Declarer Play the Bergen Way

More Declarer Play the Bergen Way

Marty Sez

Marty Sez...Volume 2

Marty Sez...Volume 3

More POINTS SCHMOINTS!

POINTS SCHMOINTS!

Bergen's Best Bridge Tips

Bergen's Best Bridge Quizzes - Volume 1

To Open, or Not to Open

Better Rebidding with Bergen

Hand Evaluation: Points, Schmoints!

Understanding 1NT Forcing

Introduction to Negative Doubles

Acknowledgments

Manuscript edited by Patty Magnus.

My very special thanks to: Cheryl Bergen, Caitlin, Chilly and Claude Cain, Don Campbell, Larry Cohen, John Collins, Ned Downey, Steve Jones, Mary and Richard Oshlag, David Pollard and Avrom Pozen.

Foreplay

I thought that might pique your interest. Good, I was afraid that if I used the technically correct term, some of you might skip this section. Please do not, there is some good stuff here.

In *Points Schmoints*, I described negative doubles as "the most important convention in modern bridge." That was certainly not the most controversial statement I have ever made. As a matter of fact, if forced to choose, I would sooner give up Stayman.

But what exactly is a negative double? Presenting a technical definition out of a textbook would not serve us well. Instead, here are some of the reasons that I find this convention indispensable when coping with an enemy overcall.

✓ Negative doubles allow responder to take action with many promising hands that lack the strength or suit length needed to bid. Once responder has shown some values, the road is paved for opener to investigate the possibility of game.

✓ Negative doubles are essential for finding four-four fits. Our ancestors had no such problems—they played four-card majors. The modern approach to bridge, which embraces five-card majors, makes us work harder.

Negative doubles have been around for a long time. *The Official Encyclopedia of Bridge* credits Alvin Roth and Tobias Stone for introducing the modern negative double to tournament play in 1957. It was nicknamed Sputnik, because the Russian space satellite dated from the same period.

Despite its history and popularity, the fact remains that no other convention results in such diverse interpretations. Prolific bridge author and World Champion Eddie Kantar went so far as to say that: regarding negative doubles, no two players are in agreement. I'll second that.

As a matter of fact, negative doubles are complicated. Back in the 1980s, my editor at *The Bridge Bulletin* suggested I do a series on the convention. I bet that he had a few months in mind. The next thing he knew, it was some three years later and there was plenty more to be discussed!

The message a negative double conveys will vary dramatically from auction to auction. The suit opened, the suit overcalled and the level of the overcall all determine its precise meaning. For example, a negative double on the auction 1♣ - (1◊) promises both majors, but after 1♣ - (3◊) it does not. Understanding this, and various other nuances, is far from trivial.

In addition, there are quite a few misconceptions about negative doubles. Here are some, all of which are incorrect.

Negative doubles deny an opening bid.
A negative double promises both unbid suits.
This double is negative: 1 suit - (1NT) - Dbl.

If you are a less experienced player, please do not be put off by the few advanced conventions included in this book. It is even okay to skip them. The bulk of information will be helpful to any player who uses negative doubles. The frills merely serve to complement the bread and butter issues. Who knows, you might even surprise yourself by adding a twist or two to your repertoire.

Bon Appétit

Marty Bergen   **April 2008**

Marty Bergen

Overview

I would like to make things as easy as possible for the most important people—you—the readers. Here is an outline that will help you get the most out of *Negative Doubles*.

The first chapter, "The Quintessential Convention," sets the scene. It answers many questions you'll have about how to play negative doubles, including: how many points do I need for the double? How high should we play them? How do we evaluate our hand for this call? On what auctions do they apply?

Does a negative double promise both unbid suits? You might be surprised at the answer to that controversial issue. In "Unbid Suits" we will get to the bottom of this.

"Opener's Rebids" will also open your eyes. You will learn that rebidding after partner makes a negative double is often more difficult than choosing a rebid in an uncontested auction.

Next comes the heart of the book. Each negative double is presented, from 1♣ - (1◇) all the way through 1♠ - (5◇). The auctions appear in order based on the rank of the opponent's overcall (which is always identified inside of parenthesis). Within this section, each auction receives an extensive, two-page, side-by-side examination.

I did include an advanced chapter which introduces a few ideas that you may find interesting. There is also a chapter of alternatives for those of you who are rather adventurous. In it you will find some Bergen originals—ideas which have never before appeared in print.

You should definitely pay special attention to the "Partnership Checklists." Because this book is oriented towards partnerships, I emphasized topics where a "meeting of the minds" is required.

The Quintessential Convention

Comparing Negative and Takeout Doubles

It is very important to know the difference between a negative double and a takeout double. This chart should give you a leg up on the subject.

Negative Double	Takeout Double
Partner opened	An opponent opened
The double is made by the responder	The double is made by the overcalling side
Overcaller's suit is doubled	Opener's suit is doubled
6+ HCP are needed at the one level, more at higher levels	11+ HCP are needed at the one level, more at higher levels
Emphasis is on the unbid major(s)	All unbid suits are promised
You need not be short in the opponent's suit	You must be short in the opponent's suit
A negative double followed by a bid in a new suit is weak	A takeout double followed by a bid in a new suit is strong (17+ HCP)

Points Needed for a Negative Double

Take a look at the following chart to get an idea of the minimum high card point (HCP) requirements needed to make a negative double.

Level of Overcall	HCP Needed
One of a suit	6
Two of a minor	8
Two of a major	9
Three of a suit	10
Four or higher of a suit	10

Now we have some numbers to work with. "Ah, but Marty Bergen doesn't bow to the point count gods," I hear you cry. Agreed. There is definitely an element of *points, schmoints* in the air. Read on to learn more.

What's the Point?

When I talk about points in this section, I am referring basically to HCP. However, good players know that:

Aggressive action is called for when:

✓ You are short in the opponent's suit,	and/or
✓ You know you have a fit,	and/or
✓ You have tolerance for opener's suit,	and/or
✓ You have ideal distribution in the unbid suit(s),	and/or
✓ You have prime cards (aces and kings).	

Discretion is recommended with:

✓ Length in the opponent's suit,	and/or
✓ Shortness in partner's suit,	and/or
✓ Flawed distribution in the unbid suits,	and/or
✓ A hand that is dominated by minor honors (queens and jacks).	

Now, take a look at one specific auction, 1◇ - (2♣), and see these principles at work. In general you should have at least eight HCP to make a negative double after a two-of-a-minor overcall.

You would be happy to double with:

♠ A765   ♡ KQ96   ◇ 832   ♣ 43
(Four cards in each major, enough points, perfect.)

However, I would also double (imperfectly) with the next two hands. Although they are sub-par in the HCP department, their positives outweigh their negatives:

♠ KJ96   ♡ Q9863   ◇ 874   ♣ 2
(We do not have eight HCP, so if partner bids notrump this hand will be a disappointment. However, the singleton club and nice major-suit distribution make the double correct.)

♠ K983   ♡ A96   ◇ 10954   ♣ 53
(You have only seven HCP and lack a fourth heart, but the diamond fit and prime cards cover you.)

On the other hand, I would not double 2♣ with:

♠ K865   ♡ A74   ◇ 7   ♣ J10872
(Pass. You have club length and a singleton in partner's suit.)

♠ QJ   ♡ 98754   ◇ Q73   ♣ QJ4
(Pass. You are unprepared for a 2♠ response and hate those overrated queens and jacks.)

How High?

One of the questions that many players ask about negative doubles is: how high should they be played? I am guessing that the most popular answer would be 3♠. The majority is stating that they treat doubles at higher levels as penalty.

Right or wrong, we will make that assumption and run with it. When I think of penalty doubles, the following comes to mind. We are happy to make a penalty double when:

✓ We have a trump stack.
✓ We have no interest in bidding on.

I do not think anyone would have a problem with those. Now, take a look at a typical auction where the "3♠ majority" mentioned above would regard responder's double as penalty.

1♠ - (4♢) - Dbl

Notice that this double is extremely unlikely to meet either of the necessary conditions. When a player jumps to the four level, there is almost no chance of another player having length and strength in that suit. A realistic hand for responder is:

♠ AJ   ♡ KJ72   ♢ 53   ♣ K9643

As opposed to:

♠ 8   ♡ A63   ♢ KQ108   ♣ Q8762

Therefore, responder's doubles at high levels should not be defined as penalty: they are also negative. Opener is free to pass, but he should not regard the double as the end of the auction.

Watch opener in action on the following auction:

1♡ - (4♠) - Dbl - (Pass)

Opener's hand is:

♠ — ♡ KQJ984 ♢ AQJ107 ♣ 65

It would be crazy to pass. Bid 5♢. Your partner has points, not a spade stack. Your hand screams offense, not defense. That would be 100% true even if you did not play negative doubles this high.

I am going to define responder's double as negative through 5♢. If you think that what you name the double is not the key issue here, you are on track. The fact remains that the higher the level of the double, the more likely that opener will leave it in. Opener's pass, however, is far from automatic. Usually, neither opener nor responder will be salivating at the thought of defending the contract that was doubled.

Non-Negative Doubles

In order to be able to play negative doubles effectively, it is crucial to identify which auctions are excluded. **Negative doubles do not apply when the opponent's overcall is in notrump or is a two-level cuebid (such as Michaels).**

Non-negative doubles show general strength. They are similar to responder's redouble after partner opens and an opponent makes a takeout double. The usual minimum is 10 HCP, although doubles after a 1NT overcall can be made with slightly less strength.

Here is a complete list of auctions where responder's double is not negative.

1 of a suit - (1NT) - Dbl

1 of a suit - (2 of same suit) - Dbl

1 of a suit - (2NT) - Dbl

1 of a suit - (3NT) - Dbl

Unbid Suits

Four Spades or Five?

Do you regard these auctions in the same light?

1♣ - (1◇) -1♠
1♣ - (1♡) -1♠

"Yes," is a very understandable answer to that question. The two auctions certainly appear to be similar. However, they must be regarded differently. Please read on.

I will begin with the second auction because it is easier to understand. Here's the scoop.

Responder could have made a negative double of 1♡ to show four spades (the only unbid major). Therefore, **the 1♠ response after 1 of a minor - (1♡) guarantees at least five spades**.

The auction 1♣ - (1◇) is another story. Responder must be careful not to encourage his partner to show a major that he may have no interest in. Therefore, he should not make a negative double unless he has both majors. For instance, wouldn't you feel silly if you made a negative double after 1♣ - (1◇) with this hand:

♠ Q3   ♡ KQ63   ◇ 8653   ♣ 942

and heard the auction proceed:

1♣ - (1◇) - Dbl - (1NT)
2♠ - (Pass) - ?

The solution is simple, just respond 1♡ at your first turn.

Here are four more hands where you should bid your major, rather than double, after 1♣ - (1◇).

♠ 7 ♡ Q1086 ◇ 7543 ♣ AQ95

♠ AJ108 ♡ 74 ◇ Q5 ♣ J7532

♠ 84 ♡ A985 ◇ 8543 ♣ KQ6

♠ K654 ♡ 842 ◇ 83 ♣ AK73

Bridge players are taught from the cradle that the requirements for responding in a major suit at the one level are very gentle: a four-card suit and six HCP. When RHO bids 1◇, just ignore the overcall and go ahead and bid your four-card major.

Does every bridge player in the world bid this way? Of course not. (Do you and your peers agree 100% on any topic?) However, I feel comfortable recommending the following:

After 1♣ - (1◇), a negative double shows at least four cards in each major. No other negative double auction makes the same promise.

If anyone tries to tell you that responding in a major after the auction 1♣ - (1◇) promises five cards, tell them no, No, NO.

1 Minor - (1 or 2 of Major)

What would you do with the following hands? In each case, you are responding to partner's opening bid.

1♦ - (1♡) - ?

♠ A643 ♡ 8754 ♦ A85 ♣ 73

♠ J853 ♡ 74 ♦ AK82 ♣ 982

1♣ - (2♠) - ?

♠ 52 ♡ AK95 ♦ Q6 ♣ Q7432

♠ J85 ♡ Q9873 ♦ 852 ♣ AQ

I hope that you found this to be easy. If not,

✓ Keep reading.
✓ Big hint: the answer to every question is identical.
✓ Very big hint: take a look at the front cover.

For all of these hands there is no second choice. You must make a negative double. The fact that you do not have the unbid minor is irrelevant and should not stop you from doubling. If I had a nickel for every time I have heard (and even read!) that a negative double promises both unbid suits, I would be a very wealthy man. No, **when partner opens in a minor and RHO's overcall is one or two of a major, a negative double promises the unbid major only. It says nothing about the unbid minor.**

14

1 Minor - (2 Other Minor)

You are still the responder. What is your call?

Our first auction is 1◇ - (2♣) - ?

♠ AQ ♡ K854 ◇ 7643 ♣ 976

♠ K6432 ♡ A8 ◇ J74 ♣ 542

♠ KQ65 ♡ A ◇ A543 ♣ 8742

Next we have 1♣ - (2◇) - ?

♠ 854 ♡ AKJ9 ◇ 7 ♣ 97543

♠ AJ63 ♡ 852 ◇ 843 ♣ AQJ

♠ AJ7 ♡ K8543 ◇ 85 ♣ 1073

Were you a persistent doubler? I certainly hope so—the alternatives were not appealing. Remember, responding in an unbid major suit at the two level promises "five and dime" (at least a five-card suit as well as 10 HCP).

However, we never had both majors for our negative double. Some players (not to mention bridge books) give us the impression that this is a big no-no. Balderdash! **After partner's minor is overcalled with the unbid minor at the two level, a negative double promises only one major.** Those who wait for a perfect double such as:

♠ AJ95 ♡ AJ95 ◇ 64 ♣ 843

will be missing far too many opportunities.

15

1 Major - (1 or 2 of Other Major)

Are you ready to respond?

1♥ - (1♠) - ?

♠ 7643   ♥ AJ   ◇ KJ754   ♣ 32

♠ 952   ♥ K7   ◇ AJ3   ♣ 107643

1♠ - (2♥) - ?

♠ J4   ♥ J43   ◇ KQ6   ♣ QJ743

♠ 43   ♥ 7532   ◇ Q10943   ♣ AK

1♥ - (2♠) - ?

♠ 843   ♥ A2   ◇ K9743   ♣ Q108

♠ J62   ♥ 84   ◇ QJ9   ♣ AQ876

Not so easy, but, once again I am consistent. On all six, make a negative double. You want to show some values, but are not strong enough to make a forcing bid at a higher level.

Of course, it would have been easy to make a negative double on any of the auctions above with this hand:

♠ 65   ♥ 43   ◇ KQJ7   ♣ K8754

So what's the catch? None of the hands above had both unbid minors. I hope that did not stop you. **You cannot wait to have both unbid suits to make a negative double unless the auction specifically begins 1♣ - (1◇).**

Suits Promised by a Negative Double

After an opening bid and overcall, there are two unbid suits. Many people believe that a negative double guarantees both. As you have learned in this chapter, that is not true. Below is a summary of this very important topic. Because responder has special considerations at higher levels, the following refers to auctions at the one and two levels only. We will defer our look at suits promised at higher levels until later.

The unbid suits are the majors; e.g., 1♢ - (2♣) - Dbl:

A negative double promises at least one major.

Remember that 1♣ - (1♢) - Dbl promises both majors.

Only one major suit is unbid; e.g., 1♠ - (2♣) - Dbl:

A negative double promises the unbid major. It says nothing about the unbid minor.

The unbid suits are the minors; e.g., 1♡ - (1♠) - Dbl:

A negative double promises at least one minor.

Responder Makes a Jump Shift in Competition

With neither side vulnerable, you hold:

♠ 765   ♡ 4   ◇ KQ108754   ♣ 43

A perfect 3◇ preempt. Unfortunately, partner is the dealer and opens 1♣. You are still well placed. You can respond 3◇ (a double jump), promising a preempt just like a 3◇ opening would.

However, your RHO chimes in with a 1♠ overcall. If you bid 3◇ now, you are making a jump shift—which is traditionally treated as strong— showing at least 17 HCP. But with those lovely diamonds you want to bid something.

Bidding 2◇ would be very misleading. You would be making a forcing, forward-going bid promising at least 10 HCP. Even if you were able to follow up with a nonforcing 3◇ bid, opener would expect a better hand.

Here is the solution. **After a simple (non-jump) overcall, define jump shifts as preemptive.** Experienced players already employ this tactic after a takeout double.

✓ If responder has 17 HCP after an opponent overcalls (quite unlikely), he should content himself by bidding his suit (forcing), intending to follow up as needed.

✓ The weak jump shift (WJS) in competition promises a weak hand with a long suit. Responder typically holds six or seven cards in the suit. His HCP range is 2-7, but he will usually be in the middle of that range.

Vulnerability is obviously relevant, but an aggressive mindset is recommended.

Here are some other examples of this bid:

After 1♣ - (1♡)

♠ KQ9863 ♡ 85 ◇ 96 ♣ 742
(Bid 2♠.)

♠ 9 ♡ 987 ◇ KQJ1092 ♣ 732
(Bid 3◇.)

The weak jump shift in competition is an essential convention that I would recommend to players at all levels. This preempt is analogous to each of the following: the weak two bid, the opening three bid and the weak jump overcall.

Opener's Rebids

Bid Your Three-Card Major Under Duress

Nobody enjoys this topic, but it must be addressed. If you have never been confronted with a situation like the following, consider yourself fortunate. You are in fourth seat with an innocuous hand:

♠ 87 ♡ QJ10 ◊ 76432 ♣ 654

The auction begins: (1◊) - Dbl - (Pass) - ?

All of a sudden, the spotlight is on you. What would you do? Obviously, you have to bid something. You are too weak for 1NT, not to mention that your diamond stopper is a trifle sketchy. The correct bid is 1♡, because all of the alternatives are a lot worse. You might even concede that it was considerate of me to deal you a suit with three honors.

Like it or not, this situation is not unique. After partner opens 1◊ and your RHO passes, what would you respond holding?

♠ KQJ ♡ 3 ◊ 865 ♣ 876432

The textbook answer is 1NT, because your hand is too weak for a 2♣ bid, too strong for a pass and you lack the four-card suit needed to bid 1♠ or 2◊. However, an expert would prefer 1♠, based on the chunky spades.

The above may or may not interest you, but the relevant question is: "what does this have to do with negative doubles?" Please read on to find out.

Okay, you have opened 1◊ and the auction now proceeds:

1◊ - (2♣) - Dbl - (Pass)

What would you bid with each of the following hands?

♠ K76 ♡ AKQ ◊ J643 ♣ J54

♠ AQJ ♡ Q5 ◊ A943 ♣ 6432

♠ AK ♡ AJ10 ◊ 10876 ♣ 8753

Your clubs are too weak to bid 2NT or to pass. See the problem? I hope that we are now reunited. If your answers to the above were anything other than 2♡, 2♠ and 2♡, respectively, I beg to differ.

Once again, I was trying to be helpful by loading up the three-card major with honors. The sad truth is that this will not always be the case.

You might believe that the problem was caused because you were at the two level. Yes it was. However, I am afraid that the one level can also be messy. After 1♣ - (1♡) - Dbl - (Pass), what should opener rebid holding:

♠ AQ10 ♡ 753 ◊ AK ♣ 98654

1NT? You do not have a heart stopper.

2♣? It is obscene to rebid that club suit.

1♠? The winner by default.

Opener Rebids a Five-Card Suit

When my students ask if they should rebid unsupported five-card suits, I tell them honestly, "It is usually wrong to do so." I stand by that advice **for noncompetitive auctions.** Here is why. Suppose you pick up:

♠ 852   ♡ 985   ♢ AK   ♣ KQ986

You open 1♣ and the auction proceeds as follows:

1♣ - (Pass) - 1♠ - (Pass)

You should rebid 1NT with your balanced minimum—you cannot afford to worry about your weak heart holding. In an uncontested auction, a 1NT rebid does not promise a stopper in every unbid suit.

Look what happens when LHO overcalls 1♠ and partner makes a negative double.

1♣ - (1♠) - Double - (Pass)

Now you should not bid 1NT because you do not have a stopper in the opponent's suit. Therefore, with the same hand, most experts would rebid 2♣. Of course, if responder had made his negative double holding a singleton club, 2♣ would not be the contract of the century.

The problem is more pronounced at the two level. If the auction began 1♡ - (2♢) - Dbl - (Pass) and I held this hand:

♠ K6   ♡ J7542   ♢ J75   ♣ AKJ

I would definitely prefer to be elsewhere but would grit my teeth and bid 3♣. On the other hand, I would rebid 2♡ with a clear conscience holding:

♠ KQ   ♡ KQJ63   ♢ J75   ♣ Q43

Opener's Strong Bids

This is a controversial area, and not everyone will agree with me. (Editor's note: what else is new?) However, it is sound advice. So here goes. After responder makes a negative double:

- ✓ A cuebid by opener is forcing to game. It says nothing about his distribution or holding in the enemy's suit.
- ✓ All jumps below game are invitational, regardless of whether responder promised that particular suit.
- ✓ Double and triple jumps to game in a major are weaker than a cuebid.
- ✓ Reverses only rear their ugly heads when you open 1♣ and later bid diamonds. A 2◇ reverse is forcing for one round. A reverse at a higher level is forcing to game.

Here are some examples to clarify. You are the opener.

What is your rebid after 1♣ - (1♡) - Dbl - (Pass)?

♠ AQ ♡ 65 ◇ AK76 ♣ A8653
(Bid 2◇. The reverse promises at least 17 points.)

♠ A ♡ A6 ◇ AK42 ♣ A98642
(2♡. We are on our way to bidding a game or slam in clubs, diamonds or notrump.)

♠ KJ96 ♡ 74 ◇ 87 ♣ AKQ53
(2♠, invitational. This is certainly a nice hand once partner has promised spades.)

♠ AQ84 ♡ 52 ◇ 94 ♣ AKQ54
(3♠. Highly invitational.)

♠ KQJ6 ♡ 95 ◇ 3 ♣ AKJ842
(4♠. You must insist on game with this shape.)

Opener Rebids Notrump

On all of these hands, you are the opener. What is your rebid after partner's negative double?

1♣ - (1♠) - Dbl - (Pass)
?

♠ 10964 ♡ J43 ◇ KQJ ♣ AQ5
(Bid 1NT. We try to have a stopper in the enemy's suit, but cannot always deliver. Although rare, it does happen.)

♠ KQJ ♡ A ◇ KJ6 ♣ A98653
(2NT. A stopper is needed, but your hand may be unbalanced.)

♠ AQ ♡ Q ◇ J65 ♣ AKQJ754
(3NT. In addition to a stopper in the opponent's suit, this double jump shows an unbalanced hand. Why unbalanced? If you have a balanced hand, you can show your values in other ways. For example, you would jump to 2NT with 18-19 HCP or open 2NT with more.)

Different auction, once again you have opened.

1◇ - (2♡) - Dbl - (Pass)
?

♠ KJ10 ♡ A8 ◇ 87653 ♣ KJ4
(2♠. Try to avoid rebidding 2NT with an absolute minimum.)

♠ AQ ♡ K76 ◇ A9865 ♣ KQ8
(3NT. This is a classic.)

♠ K ♡ AQ5 ◇ AK8542 ♣ J105
(3NT. This single jump to 3NT is sometimes made with an unbalanced hand.)

Reopening Doubles

If you do not know what a "trap" pass is, you are missing out. Responder makes a trap pass of an opponent's overcall with a nice hand that includes length and strength in the enemy's suit. Shortness in partner's suit also suggests trying for penalties.

Experienced responders are prepared to trap pass even at the one level. If opener is able to balance with a takeout double, a bonanza may be forthcoming.

For example, after 1◇ - (1♠) it is correct to pass with:

♠ KJ1087 ♡ AJ42 ◇ 8 ♣ J85

You hope that opener will balance with a double. Because responder's pass will sometimes be setting the trap, so to speak, opener will strive to balance with a double (takeout) after:

1 of a suit - (overcall) - Pass - (Pass)

Once opener does balance with a double, responder will gladly pass with hands similar to the one above.

It would, however, be overreacting for opener to always double "just in case." For example, the auction begins:

1♠ - (2♣) - Pass - (Pass)

As opener you have:

♠ KQ8754 ♡ KQJ64 ◇ 65 ♣ —

You should bid 2♡ instead of doubling. Of course, if partner has trap passed with:

♠ 9 ♡ 53 ◇ AQJ4 ♣ QJ10986

he will be more than slightly disappointed. That's life.

25

When deciding whether or not to reopen with a double, it is essential that opener examine his holding in the opponent's suit. Here are some guidelines:

Opener's Holding in the Enemy's Suit	When to Double
Void	Do not make a balancing double with a void unless there is no alternative. Defending with a trump void is rarely correct.
Singleton	Ideal time to double. Strive to do so unless you have an extremely unbalanced hand with limited defense.
Doubleton	Good time to double, especially when the overcall is at a low level.
Three Cards	Try to avoid making a takeout double with more than two cards in the opponent's suit.
Four to Five Cards	Opener should never double here.

Here are some examples to clarify the concepts above. The auction proceeds 1♠ - (2♣) - Pass - (Pass) and it is opener's turn.

♠ AJ6532 ♡ A8 ◇ A742 ♣ 6
(Double. With all this defense, I sure hope partner can pass for penalties. If he responds 2♡, you have an easy 2♠ rebid.)

♠ KQJ65 ♡ A10954 ◇ A7 ♣ 4
(Double. Your hearts can wait. Your first priority is to give partner a chance to pass and take the opponents for a ride. Failing that, you can always bid 2♡ over 2◇.)

The Penalty Pass

You hold:

♠ A ♡ KJ975 ◇ 865 ♣ K743

The auction proceeds:

West	You	East	South
3♡	Pass	Pass	Dbl
Pass	?		

YES! Pass like a shot. I live for this!

The pass of partner's takeout double is referred to as a penalty pass. With the hand above, it is indescribably delicious.

The penalty pass plays an important role for opener after partner has made a negative double. You open 1♡ with the following hand:

♠ 7 ♡ K9864 ◇ A52 ♣ AKJ9

The auction proceeds:

You	North	East	South
1♡	2♣	Dbl	Pass
?			

You have terrific clubs and are delighted to pass.

This hand represents the exception rather than the rule at low levels. When you open one of a suit, it is very unlikely that you will have a massive holding in your opponent's suit.

At higher levels, opener will be forced to make a penalty pass of partner's negative double with very modest trump holdings. For example, the auction begins:

You	North	East	South
1♣	3♠	Dbl	Pass
?			

Your hand is:

♠ 432 ♡ 653 ◇ AKJ ♣ AJ42

I see no alternative to making a penalty pass despite my "magnificent" spade holding of 432.

Here is some advice for opener after partner's negative double:

Level	Likelihood of Passing	Typical Trump Holding for Pass	Do Not Pass with this # of Trumps
1	Almost never	AQJ10	4, usually
2	Rare	KQJ8	3
3	Sometimes	10876	2
4 minor	Almost always if balanced	Q52	1
4 major	Always if balanced	J64	void
5	Almost always	83	0, 1 with great shape

Stop—Read This

With our background debriefing out of the way, we are now ready to address the heart of *Negative Doubles*. To get you started, I would like to explain the format of the pages that follow so you can get the most out of the material presented.

For each auction, there are two facing pages which go hand in hand. The opponent's overcall (in parenthesis) will not vary on those pages. However, opener's bid sometimes will. This was done so that I could make the point that the principles involved were not dependent on which minor or major was opened.

The left-hand page begins with an explanation of what is required for a negative double on each auction featured at the top of the page. Next, there are three sets of sample hands. The first shows examples of "perfect negative doubles." The second gives some "imperfect negatives doubles," while the last set presents hands where you should not double at all.

Explanations are provided in this section for clarification where needed. However, you can work with the sample hands in a few ways. You might choose to test yourself by covering up the answers or you might prefer to "just read." Your choice.

The left-hand page concludes with what I have described as "worth noting." Sometimes you will find an original tidbit and at other times there will be a review of a particularly important idea.

The right-hand page in these chapters focuses on opener's rebids after the negative double. My goal was to provide a mixture of straightforward and challenging examples. I also included a checkmarked list to remind you of the principles being discussed.

Negative Doubles at the One Level

1♣ - (1♢) - Dbl

This negative double guarantees at least 4-4 in the majors and 6+ HCP. However, with nine or more cards in the majors and an opening bid or better, responder should bid rather than double.

Perfect doubles:

♠ A765 ♡ K643 ♢ 74 ♣ 943

♠ KJ64 ♡ K654 ♢ A53 ♣ K7
(There is no upper limit on the strength of a negative double.)

Imperfect double:

♠ QJ87 ♡ QJ87 ♢ 9654 ♣ Q
(This is an ugly hand with a club misfit, no aces or kings and length in the enemy's suit. But with 4-4 in the majors, double.)

Do not double with:

♠ AQ965 ♡ AQ643 ♢ 65 ♣ 5
(Respond 1♠ with this good hand and 5-5 distribution.)

♠ 6532 ♡ KQ10965 ♢ 75 ♣ 3
(A weak jump shift of 2♡ says it all.)

♠ K642 ♡ K1074 ♢ AJ1083 ♣ —
(Pass. Even at the one level, a trap pass can be quite lucrative.)

Worth noting: responder's bid in a major after 1♣ - (1♢) does not promise a five-card suit.

Opener Rebids after 1♣ - (1◇) - Dbl - (Pass)

✓ A cuebid is forcing to game.
✓ All jumps below game are invitational.
✓ 1NT usually promises a stopper in overcaller's suit
✓ Opener may be forced to rebid a five-card suit or introduce a three-card suit.
✓ A double jump to 3NT shows length and strength in the suit opened and a big hand, as well as the necessary stopper in the opponent's suit.
✓ Double and triple jumps to game in a major are weaker than a cuebid followed by a jump to game.

Bid 1♡ with: ♠ KJ ♡ 9654 ◇ A87 ♣ KQ53

1♠ with: ♠ KQJ ♡ Q54 ◇ 987 ♣ AJ53
(Strong three-card majors may be bid here when stuck.)

2◇ with: ♠ AK54 ♡ A ◇ 876 ♣ AKJ54
(Opener's cuebid after a negative double is forcing to game.)

2♡ with: ♠ A4 ♡ AQ108 ◇ 864 ♣ A765
(This promises a better hand than a 1♡ bid.)

2NT with: ♠ AQ5 ♡ KJ7 ◇ AQ ♣ Q8654

3♠ with: ♠ AQJ4 ♡ AJ ◇ 63 ♣ KJ1054
(Highly invitational, just like jump-raising a 1♠ response.)

3NT with: ♠ A7 ♡ 83 ◇ K7 ♣ AKQ8654

4♡ with: ♠ 7 ♡ AQJ7 ◇ 83 ♣ AK9765

1♣ - (1♡) - Dbl

This auction guarantees precisely four spades, and at least six HCP. It says nothing about the unbid minor. If the opening bid is 1◇, nothing changes.

Perfect doubles:

♠ A876   ♡ 64   ◇ A643   ♣ 854

Imperfect doubles:

♠ J643   ♡ A1093   ◇ Q974   ♣ 5
(I am not thrilled with my potential club misfit and good defense. However, I would still double with my four spades and seven HCP.)

♠ 10953   ♡ 63   ◇ K7   ♣ AKQJ3
(Your magnificent clubs might appear to be more noteworthy than your modest spades, but majors take precedence.)

Do not double with:

♠ K7643   ♡ A4   ◇ J74   ♣ Q92
(Bid 1♠ because you have five of them.)

♠ 9432   ♡ KJ1094   ◇ Q4   ♣ J4
(Pass with these terrific hearts in an otherwise lousy hand.)

♠ A742   ♡ 74   ◇ AQ1072   ♣ A4
(Bid 2◇. Your bid of a new suit at the two level does not deny four spades. When you bid spades later, you will be showing a hand with opening bid strength. Change the ♣A to the ♣2 and you would prefer to make a negative double.)

Worth noting: if responder does not make a negative double, but bids 1NT instead, he denies four spades.

Opener Rebids after 1♢ - (1♡) - Dbl - (Pass)

Bid 1NT with: ♠ 654 ♡ J108 ♢ AKJ6 ♣ A74
(Any better ideas? We try to have a stopper, but when you're stuck, you're stuck.)

2♣ with: ♠ AK ♡ 542 ♢ 97542 ♣ KQJ
(2♣ is superior to 1NT because our clubs are so strong. As for 2♢, I cannot discuss that in mixed company.)

2♢ with: ♠ 87 ♡ A3 ♢ AQ8654 ♣ QJ3

2♡ with: ♠ K ♡ A3 ♢ AKJ754 ♣ KQ92
(En route to game or slam somewhere.)

2♠ with: ♠ AQ72 ♡ 53 ♢ AK754 ♣ 82

2NT with: ♠ AQ ♡ KJ7 ♢ AKQ2 ♣ 9654

3♣ with: ♠ A3 ♡ 8 ♢ KQJ76 ♣ KQ1087
(Opener's jump shift after a negative double is invitational.)

3♢ with: ♠ K73 ♡ 87 ♢ AKJ1085 ♣ A3

3♠ with: ♠ AQ32 ♡ A82 ♢ J7654 ♣ A

3NT with: ♠ Q73 ♡ KJ ♢ AKQ1074 ♣ A6

4♠ with   ♠ KQ104 ♡ 8 ♢ KQJ754 ♣ KJ

1♦ - (1♠) - Dbl

When responder doubles a spade overcall to shows hearts, we have the essence of the negative double. Responder guarantees at least four hearts and 6+ HCP. It is possible for responder to have a longer heart suit because he needs a good hand (with 10+ HCP) to respond 2♡. These concepts also apply if partner opens 1♣.

Perfect doubles:

♠ 87   ♡ KQ54   ♢ Q954   ♣ 965
(You have four hearts—do not worry about clubs.)

♠ 6   ♡ A1074   ♢ K743   ♣ Q952

Imperfect doubles:

♠ 986   ♡ A8653   ♢ KJ   ♣ 852
(You have no way to show the fifth heart because a direct 2♡ bid would be forcing.)

♠ 64   ♡ J75432   ♢ AQ   ♣ 1098
(You hope to be able to bid 2♡ at your next turn.)

Do not double with:

♠ 86   ♡ KQJ93   ♢ A1087   ♣ 96
(You have the requisite 10 HCP and are delighted to bid 2♡.)

Worth noting: responder's double says nothing about his holding in the unbid minor. The double merely states that responder would have bid 1♡ without the intervening spade bid.

Opener Rebids after 1♣ - (1♠) - Dbl - (Pass)

Bid 1NT with: ♠ Q98 ♡ A4 ◇ KQJ ♣ J7643

2♣ with: ♠ 754 ♡ AK ◇ 643 ♣ AQ1098
(Although you have only five clubs, the spots are great. Rebid them rather than venture to 1NT without a spade stopper.)

2◇ with: ♠ 87 ♡ A4 ◇ AQJ3 ♣ AQ632
(I treat this as a reverse, forcing for one round. If the ♡A were the ♡2, I would have opened 1◇.)

2♡ with: ♠ 854 ♡ KQJ ◇ AK ♣ 75432
(I do not like to respond with only three hearts, but it seems best because our hearts are spectacular, and we have no spade stopper.)

2♠ with: ♠ A765 ♡ — ◇ AK8 ♣ AQJ654

3♣ with: ♠ A ♡ Q76 ◇ Q4 ♣ AQJ10976

3♡ with: ♠ 9 ♡ AJ104 ◇ A96 ♣ KQ985
(This jump is invitational. I love 5-4-3-1 hands—they are very underrated.)

3NT with: ♠ AQ ♡ J ◇ 987 ♣ AKQJ1087
(With a normal spade lead, you know you will make this even before you see the dummy.)

4♡ with: ♠ A4 ♡ AQ107 ◇ 5 ♣ A108754
(With 6-4, bid more.)

1♡ - (1♠) - Dbl

Responder denies three hearts, but does not promise both minors. You need at least six HCP for this negative double.

Perfect doubles:

♠ 96 ♡ K4 ◊ Q9653 ♣ K754

♠ 765 ♡ J6 ◊ A743 ♣ Q1074

Imperfect doubles:

♠ 854 ♡ A6 ◊ KJ ♣ 987543
(If opener responds 2◊, you will take a preference to 2♡.)

♠ 9763 ♡ A ◊ Q87543 ♣ Q10
(I never love to double when I have a long suit but I cannot bid 2◊ without 10 HCP.)

Do not double with:

♠ AQ6 ♡ 64 ◊ Q874 ♣ J765
(1NT is much more descriptive.)

♠ 64 ♡ AQ ◊ K865 ♣ A8643
(Bid 2♣. You have enough to force.)

Worth noting: after an overcall, responder's jump to 2NT should be invitational and show approximately 11 HCP. Responder should have exactly two hearts for this bid. This hand is perfect.

♠ KJ7 ♡ A6 ◊ Q842 ♣ J754

Opener Rebids after 1♡ - (1♠) - Dbl - (Pass)

Pass with: ♠ AKJ10 ♡ KQ842 ◇ K ♣ 875
(Hands with 100 honors in the enemy's suit do not grow on trees.)

Bid 1NT with: ♠ 1065 ♡ A9643 ◇ J54 ♣ AK
(What else can you do? Remember, we agreed that a "stopperless 1NT" could be rebid when stuck.)

2♣ with: ♠ 76 ♡ AQ743 ◇ 876 ♣ AQ10
(Bidding a three-card minor is sometimes the lesser of evils.)

2◇ with: ♠ Q7 ♡ K7543 ◇ AQ43 ♣ Q4

2♠ with: ♠ A7 ♡ AK8654 ◇ J ♣ KQJ5
(You are much too good for 3♣. After a negative double, a jump shift is invitational. With this gorgeous hand, you do not need too much from partner to make a club slam.)

3♣ with: ♠ A2 ♡ AK876 ◇ 94 ♣ AJ82
(An invitational 3♣ bid describes this hand.)

3◇ with: ♠ 75 ♡ AJ754 ◇ AQ432 ♣ A

3NT with: ♠ KJ ♡ AKQJ65 ◇ A7 ♣ 984
(This bid shows a terrific suit, along with the obvious spade stopper and a strong hand.)

4♡ with: ♠ 8 ♡ KQJ9765 ◇ 76 ♣ AKJ
(Do not take any chances. You have too much offense to merely invite a game.)

A Negative Double with a Six-Card Suit

Lead: ♠10

North
♠ A5
♡ AKQ
◇ K8765
♣ K76

West
♠ 10982
♡ 986
◇ QJ10
♣ J52

East
♠ KQ7643
♡ 10
◇ 43
♣ AQ104

South
♠ J
♡ J75432
◇ A92
♣ 983

West	North	East	South
—	1◇	1♠	Dbl
Pass	2NT	Pass	3♡
Pass	4♡	All pass	

After 1◇ - (1♠), South was not strong enough to bid 2♡, so he put his hearts on hold and settled for a negative double. However, once North showed a strong hand, it was safe for South to bid 3♡ to show extra length.

Declarer needs to establish diamonds without giving West the opportunity to lead through dummy's ♣K. Therefore, he must duck the opening lead to East. Upon winning, East has nothing better to do than exit with a spade. Declarer is careful to discard a diamond, not a club. It is now easy to set up dummy's diamonds by ruffing the third round, South draws trumps and enjoys dummy's last two diamond winners. 4♡, making five.

Negative Doubles at the Two Level

Lead: ♡K

North
♠ 10
♡ 7643
♢ AKQ82
♣ 1098

West
♠ KJ6
♡ KQJ102
♢ 9
♣ J762

East
♠ 9872
♡ 98
♢ 1053
♣ K543

South
♠ AQ543
♡ A5
♢ J764
♣ AQ

West	North	East	South
—	—	—	1♠
2♡	Dbl	Pass	3NT
All Pass			

North did not enjoy making a negative double with length in the opponent's suit, but he needed to show his values. With 17 HCP, South had to be in game, so he jumped to 3NT.

Declarer wanted to avoid taking a club or spade finesse for his ninth trick. He found a neat solution. He won the second heart, noting that East had two, and led diamonds until West showed out. It was now easy to throw West in with a heart, knowing that he had only three remaining. Once West finished cashing his winners, he was endplayed—forced to give declarer a ninth trick by leading a spade or a club into declarer's pair of ace-queens.

1◊ - (2♣) - Dbl

This negative double usually shows at least eight HCP and only guarantees one major (analogous to Stayman).

Perfect doubles:

♠ KJ75 ♡ A954 ◊ J65 ♣ 82

♠ AQ98 ♡ AK87 ◊ 9543 ♣ 8

Imperfect doubles:

♠ A9854 ♡ KQ7 ◊ 98 ♣ 865
(If opener bids 2♡, I will pass and wish him luck. Doubling then bidding 2♠ shows a better or longer suit than you have.)

♠ A2 ♡ KQ75 ◊ J643 ♣ 732
(If opener bids spades, we will return to diamonds.)

Do not double with:

♠ QJ10976 ♡ 7 ◊ K76 ♣ 865
(A weak jump shift of 3♠ is more descriptive.)

♠ Q72 ♡ Q7643 ◊ 8 ♣ KJ98
(Pass. You have length and strength in clubs, a weak hand and a misfit for partner's diamonds.)

Worth noting: responder's jump to three of an unbid suit is a weak jump shift. It shows six or seven cards in the suit bid, usually with 3-7 HCP.

Opener Rebids after 1◇ - (2♣) - Dbl - (Pass)

✓ A cuebid is forcing to game.
✓ All jumps below game are invitational.
✓ 2NT guarantees a stopper in the opponent's suit. Try to avoid this bid with a dead minimum.
✓ Opener may be forced to rebid a five-card suit or introduce a three-card suit.
✓ You may or may not have balanced distribution when you jump to 3NT.
✓ A double jump to game in a major promises great shape, not great strength. It is weaker than a cuebid.

Bid 2◇ with: ♠ J76   ♡ AK   ◇ KQ654   ♣ 976

2♡ with: ♠ KJ   ♡ AJ76   ◇ A7643   ♣ 98

2♠ with: ♠ AKJ   ♡ 954   ◇ KJ65   ♣ J53

2NT with: ♠ 865   ♡ 743   ◇ AKJ7   ♣ AQ6

3♣ with: ♠ A2   ♡ AKJ8   ◇ AK743   ♣ 87
(You must cuebid to tell partner that you have a great hand.)

3♠ with: ♠ AK76   ♡ J6   ◇ AK1097   ♣ 42

3NT with: ♠ AQ   ♡ J65   ◇ AJ743   ♣ KQJ
(Opener's single jump to 3NT may be based on a balanced hand.)

4♡ with: ♠ K5   ♡ KQJ6   ◇ KQJ765   ♣ 9
(Since responder did not guarantee hearts, we must have great hearts as well as six diamonds for this bid.)

1♠ - (2♣) - Dbl

This negative double guarantees at least four cards in the unbid major, and 8+ HCP. It denies three-card support for opener's major, but says nothing about the unbid minor (diamonds). If the opening bid is 1♡, the above is still true.

Perfect double:

   ♠ A4 ♡ KJ54 ◇ J8754 ♣ 64

Imperfect doubles:

   ♠ 7 ♡ AQ65 ◇ KJ65 ♣ 9542
   (The flaws are the singleton spade and club length.)

   ♠ J ♡ 8752 ◇ AQ8654 ♣ J10
   (Again, you would prefer to have two spades, and your hearts are very weak. Double anyway.)

   ♠ A ♡ J87543 ◇ K86 ♣ 532
   (Alas—I am too weak to bid my hearts now. I hope to show them later.)

Do not double with:

   ♠ K ♡ A965 ◇ AQ8652 ♣ 75
   (Bid 2◇. Bid naturally with a good hand like this one.)

   ♠ — ♡ 5432 ◇ QJ10965 ♣ A64
   (With a spade void and emaciated hearts, the weak jump shift of 3◇ seems more practical.)

Worth noting: unless responder is very short in the opponent's suit, he should avoid doubling with marginal hands.

Opener Rebids after 1♡ - (2♣) - Dbl - (Pass)

Pass with: ♠ J ♡ KQJ76 ◇ 83 ♣ AJ1076
(Dreaming, I'm always dreaming.)

Bid 2◇ with: ♠ 87 ♡ K8654 ◇ AKQ ♣ 942

2♡ with: ♠ 876 ♡ KQJ109 ◇ AK ♣ 983
(It is nice when your five-card suit looks like six.)

2NT with: ♠ A3 ♡ AQ654 ◇ 976 ♣ A105

3♣ with: ♠ AQ ♡ AQ6532 ◇ K76 ♣ A3

3◇ with: ♠ K ♡ AKQ65 ◇ KJ765 ♣ 97
(Nice hand. This hand is too good for a mere 2◇ bid, but too weak
for a cuebid.)

3♠ with: ♠ K983 ♡ KQJ76 ◇ AQ ♣ 95

3NT with: ♠ QJ ♡ AK643 ◇ KJ7 ♣ KJ6

4♡ with: ♠ AQ5 ♡ AKJ10876 ◇ 96 ♣ 9

4♠ with: ♠ KJ109 ♡ A76543 ◇ A74 ♣ —
(*Points, schmoints.* I can always be seduced by a pretty void.)

1♣ - (2♦) - Dbl

This situation is very similar to 1♦ - (2♣) - Dbl. Responder guarantees 8+ HCP and promises at least one four-card major. With shortness in the opponent's suit, responder must try hard not to pass.

Perfect doubles:

♠ QJ76 ♡ KQJ6 ♦ 75 ♣ K54

♠ A643 ♡ A865 ♦ 6 ♣ J743

Imperfect doubles:

♠ AQ109 ♡ 8762 ♦ 5 ♣ 9532
(If partner bids notrump, your six HCP will be disappointing, but you should not pass with a singleton diamond.)

♠ K4 ♡ A8543 ♦ 75 ♣ J1086
(If partner bids spades, you will preference to clubs.)

Do not double with:

♠ A543 ♡ 7542 ♦ AQ98 ♣ J
(Pass. You have great diamonds and a misfit for partner. Won't it be nice if 2♦ doubled becomes the final contract?)

Worth noting: responder's 3♦ cuebid (instead of the negative double) would promise an opening bid with good support for opener's minor, while denying a major.

Opener Rebids after 1♣ - (2◇) - Dbl - (Pass)

Pass with: ♠ —   ♡ AJ3   ◇ AK109   ♣ 986532

Bid 2♡ with: ♠ A   ♡ J765   ◇ KQJ   ♣ Q8743
(It sure is nice to have a four-card major to bid.)

2NT with: ♠ AQ   ♡ J76   ◇ AJ10   ♣ J10943

3♣ with: ♠ A2   ♡ 986   ◇ 76   ♣ AKJ765

3◇ with: ♠ A6   ♡ AJ8   ◇ 86   ♣ AKQ653
(Tough hand. If partner bids three of a major, the best you can do is bid 4♣. If partner bids 3NT, you will count your lucky stars.)

3♡ with: ♠ 98   ♡ KQ53   ◇ A   ♣ A108752
(Invitational. Your shape is more impressive than your HCP.)

3♠ with: ♠ QJ43   ♡ 4   ◇ A96   ♣ AK973

3NT with: ♠ 54   ♡ K4   ◇ KQ10   ♣ AKQ654
(You cannot afford to worry about a sneak attack in spades.)

4♣ with: ♠ K6   ♡ —   ◇ A65   ♣ KQJ98653
(Voluntarily going past 3NT shows amazing distribution.)

4♠ with: ♠ AKJ8   ♡ 9   ◇ 87   ♣ AQ10542

1♡ - (2◇) - Dbl

This situation is similar to 1♡ - (2♣) - Dbl. Responder lacks support for opener's major but promises the unbid major and 8+ HCP. The double says nothing about responder's minor suit. If partner opens 1♠, our principles remain intact.

Perfect doubles:

♠ KQ85　♡ K4　◇ 83　♣ 97654

♠ AQ43　♡ A6　◇ 876　♣ AQ87
(You can have unlimited strength for a negative double. Because we have only four spades, we cannot bid 2♠.)

Imperfect doubles:

♠ AKJ85　♡ 53　◇ 865　♣ 854
(Alas, not strong enough for 2♠.)

♠ AQ76　♡ J　◇ 6543　♣ Q854
(I would be happier with two hearts and only three diamonds.)

Do not double with:

♠ AKJ1087　♡ 76　◇ 7　♣ 9543
(Bid 2♠ despite your eight HCP. This is a promising hand.)

♠ KQ73　♡ J　◇ KJ92　♣ J742
(Trap pass. We would love to hear partner make a reopening double so we can make a penalty pass.)

Worth noting: with 6-10 points, three hearts and four or five spades, responder should raise to 2♡.With a known fit in a major, he should look no further.

Opener Rebids after 1♠ - (2◇) - Dbl - (Pass)

Bid 2♡ with: ♠ A7654 ♡ KQ10 ◇ 765 ♣ K7
(We have no alternative to bidding the three-card suit.)

2♠ with: ♠ Q75432 ♡ AK ◇ 85 ♣ AK7
(Even though you have 16 HCP, your spades are too weak for a
jump to 3♠.)

3♣ with: ♠ AJ765 ♡ 98 ◇ 96 ♣ AQJ6
(Obvious even though partner did not promise clubs.)

Also bid 3♣ with: ♠ A8753 ♡ Q84 ◇ 7 ♣ AQ73
(Only bid a three-card suit when you have no other bid to make.)

3◇ with: ♠ AQ6543 ♡ AKJ ◇ 9 ♣ A86
(We will play game or slam somewhere.)

3♡ with: ♠ AJ754 ♡ KQ105 ◇ A2 ♣ 76
(We do not need as much to invite in a suit partner promised as we
do in a suit he did not show.)

3NT with: ♠ KJ765 ♡ AQ ◇ AJ7 ♣ K76

4♣ with: ♠ KJ7653 ♡ A ◇ 9 ♣ KQJ65
(Inviting, based on your great shape.)

4♡ with: ♠ A7654 ♡ AQJ76 ◇ 9 ♣ 76
(Once partner promised four hearts and some values, we should
have very few losers.)

4♠ with: ♠ AQJ10765 ♡ A ◇ 7 ♣ Q1096
(You rate to make this unless partner has horrible clubs.)

1♦ - (2♡) - Dbl

Responder promises four or more spades and should have at least nine HCP. If partner opens 1♣, nothing changes.

Perfect doubles:

♠ KJ64 ♡ A8 ♦ KJ5 ♣ Q965

♠ AQ87 ♡ 6 ♦ K965 ♣ 7543

Imperfect doubles:

♠ AQ754 ♡ 653 ♦ J6 ♣ Q76
(I am never happy to make a negative double with a five-card major, but this hand just does not warrant a forcing 2♠ bid.)

♠ 10964 ♡ 5 ♦ A87 ♣ K9643
(I would like more HCP, but there is no way I am passing 2♡ with a singleton in the enemy's suit and some values.)

Do not double with:

♠ 6532 ♡ AQ10 ♦ Q85 ♣ Q73
(Bid 2NT. Although you are supposed to make a negative double with four cards in the unbid major, I refuse to do so with horrible spades, strong hearts, and 4-3-3-3 distribution.)

Worth noting: even at the two level, a reopening double does not promise more than a minimum hand. After the auction begins 1♦ - (2♡) - Pass - (Pass), opener would be happy to double with:

♠ KQ53 ♡ 5 ♦ AQJ4 ♣ 8763

Opener Rebids after 1♣ - (2♡) - Dbl - (Pass)

✓ A cuebid is forcing to game.
✓ All jumps below game are invitational.
✓ 2NT guarantees a stopper in the opponent's suit. Try to avoid this bid with a dead minimum.
✓ You may or may not have balanced distribution when you jump to 3NT.
✓ A double jump to game in a major promises great shape, not great strength. It is weaker than a cuebid.
✓ A reverse at the three level is forcing to game.

Bid 2♠ with:　　　　　♠ AQ9　♡ 875　◇ AQ3　♣ J754

2NT with:　　　　　　♠ J7　♡ AQ3　◇ KQ6　♣ Q8643

3♣ with:　　　　　　♠ A2　♡ 98　◇ 8654　♣ AKJ85
(You would need a very big hand to reverse to 3◇.)

3◇ with:　　　　　　♠ A42　♡ 8　◇ AKQ5　♣ AJ876
(This is the hand for a game-forcing reverse. Although 3♡ would also be forcing to game, it would be less descriptive.)

3♡ with:　　　　　　♠ A　♡ 876　◇ K76　♣ AKQJ52
(After your cuebid, partner should bid 3NT with a heart stopper. That is his first priority.)

3♠ with:　　　　　　♠ A963　♡ A5　◇ A6　♣ Q10762

3NT with:　　　　　　♠ 87　♡ A109　◇ K4　♣ AKQ643

4♠ with:　　　　　　♠ KQJ8　♡ 74　◇ 8　♣ AK9876
(With 6-4 distribution and great suits, you will take a lot of tricks.)

1♠ - (2♡) - Dbl

Responder's double denies support for opener's spades. We try to have at least nine HCP for this double, which promises at least one four-card (or longer) minor.

Perfect double:

♠ 97   ♡ 43   ◇ A7543   ♣ KQJ9

Imperfect doubles:

♠ A   ♡ 8743   ◇ AQ54   ♣ 10943
(We have too many hearts and not enough spades. At least our spade is a nice one and we have both minors.)

♠ 76   ♡ J7   ◇ J87   ♣ AK9872
(This hand is too weak for a game-forcing response of 3♣.)

Do not double with:

♠ 8   ♡ AQJ9   ◇ J643   ♣ J876
(Pass. Great hearts, lousy minors. Defend.)

♠ Q9   ♡ AQ   ◇ AJ76   ♣ 87643
(3NT is more to the point than anything else.)

Worth noting: responder's jump to 4♠ is still weak here, just as if the auction had gone 1♠ - (Pass) - 4♠.

Opener Rebids after 1♠ - (2♡) - Dbl - (Pass)

Pass with: ♠ A9765 ♡ AK98 ◇ A ♣ 743
(You certainly have a lot of defense.)

Bid 2♠ with: ♠ KJ1062 ♡ K74 ◇ AJ ♣ 932
(Avoid bidding 2NT with a minimum whenever possible.)

2NT with: ♠ Q7432 ♡ AQ9 ◇ AQ ♣ 1074

3♣ with: ♠ A5432 ♡ 984 ◇ 87 ♣ AKJ
(Bidding these chunky clubs is more appetizing than rebidding that anemic spade suit.)

3◇ with: ♠ A8764 ♡ 82 ◇ AKJ7 ♣ J5
(Nice and painless.)

3♡ with: ♠ Q98754 ♡ 9 ◇ AKQ ♣ AK7

3♠ with: ♠ AQ10864 ♡ 64 ◇ AJ7 ♣ A4

3NT with: ♠ AKJ72 ♡ AQ ◇ KJ ♣ 8643

4♣ with: ♠ A8643 ♡ 82 ◇ Q ♣ AKQ64
(Natural and invitational.)

4♠ with: ♠ KQJ109654 ♡ Q ◇ Q76 ♣ A

1♣ - (2♠) - Dbl

Responder guarantees at least four hearts and 9+ HCP. He should tread lightly because he is forcing opener to 2NT or the three level. Partner can open 1◇ and nothing changes.

Perfect doubles:

♠ 7 ♡ A754 ◇ AJ76 ♣ 8743

♠ 64 ♡ Q986 ◇ KJ4 ♣ AQ85

Imperfect double:

♠ Q4 ♡ A106542 ◇ Q7 ♣ J72
(You are just not good enough to force by bidding 3♡.)

Do not double with:

♠ — ♡ KQ1086 ◇ A10965 ♣ 865
(Bid 3♡. With great distribution highlighted by the void and two nice suits, this is no time to be worrying about HCP.)

Worth noting: after a negative double, responder's bid in a new suit is only forcing if opener has shown extra values. The following 3◇ bid is not forward going.

West	North	East	South
1♣	2♠	Dbl	Pass
2NT	Pass	3◇	

This would be a typical hand for East.

♠ 6 ♡ AJ97 ◇ QJ10765 ♣ 42

Opener Rebids after 1♦ - (2♠) - Dbl - (Pass)

Pass with: ♠ AKJ8 ♡ 7 ♦ A8754 ♣ A63
("Make them pay.")

Bid 2NT with: ♠ Q72 ♡ AK ♦ A8653 ♣ 853
(I sure hope that I have a spade stopper.)

3♣ with: ♠ 76 ♡ A9 ♦ AKQ7 ♣ 98543
(We opened 1♦ so we could bid clubs without reversing.)

3♦ with: ♠ 4 ♡ A54 ♦ KJ7543 ♣ A98
(That was easy.)

3♡ with: ♠ 863 ♡ AQ32 ♦ AQ32 ♣ 84

Also bid 3♡ with: ♠ J5 ♡ AQ10 ♦ Q8642 ♣ A73
(With notrump out of the question, I had three suits to choose
from. The heart suit was strongest, it won.)

3♠ with: ♠ 76 ♡ A3 ♦ A87543 ♣ AKQ

3NT with: ♠ A2 ♡ A4 ♦ AKQ65 ♣ 8643

4♣ with: ♠ 8 ♡ A ♦ K87653 ♣ AJ1086
(You can afford to invite because of your great shape.)

4♡ with: ♠ 98 ♡ AK76 ♦ AKJ96 ♣ 52

1♡ - (2♠) - Dbl

This negative double denies three hearts. However, because opener will usually be bidding at the three level, responder should not double capriciously. Nine HCP is the usual minimum.

Perfect double:

♠ 95 ♡ J5 ◇ KQJ6 ♣ K9765

Imperfect doubles:

♠ 863 ♡ K6 ◇ AQ10984 ♣ 86
(If partner responds 3♣, we will bid 3◇ and hope for the best. I hate being preempted.)

♠ J54 ♡ K ◇ AJ5 ♣ J86542
(I am not happy making a negative double with the singleton heart, spade "length" or concealed six-card suit. However, with ten HCP I must take action.)

Do not double with:

♠ KJ3 ♡ 64 ◇ Q754 ♣ AJ84
(2NT is a perfectly descriptive natural bid.)

♠ 54 ♡ K5 ◇ AJ65 ♣ AQ632
(Respond 3♣, forcing to game.)

Worth noting: after 1♡ - (2♠), a jump to 4♡ by responder would show heart support, but is not weak. Remember, you cannot "preempt a preempt." This bid shows roughly 12 points, including distribution, and at least three hearts.

Opener Rebids after 1♡ - (2♠) - Dbl - (Pass)

Bid 3♣ with: ♠ 63 ♡ J87643 ◇ A ♣ AQ74
(Because partner may have fewer than two hearts, it is sensible to get clubs into the picture.)

Also bid 3♣ with: ♠ A5 ♡ A7543 ◇ A6 ♣ 6532
(Aces and spaces play better in a suit contract than in notrump.)

3◇ with: ♠ A93 ♡ AKJ76 ◇ J765 ♣ 9

3♡ with: ♠ 842 ♡ AKJ109 ◇ KJ ♣ J75
(It is rare to rebid an unsupported five-card major at the three level, but look at those hearts.)

Also bid 3♡ with: ♠ KQ ♡ QJ10865 ◇ 9 ♣ A1053
(This looks like a rebiddable suit to me.)

3♠ with: ♠ 64 ♡ AK864 ◇ AK65 ♣ K7

3NT with: ♠ QJ9 ♡ QJ873 ◇ A ♣ AKJ9
(I hope we did not belong in clubs.)

4♣ with: ♠ 4 ♡ A96432 ◇ A ♣ KJ843
("Six-five, come alive.")

4♡ with: ♠ 9 ♡ AQJ1093 ◇ Q743 ♣ AQ
(Your hearts should be good enough even if partner is void.)

Negative Doubles at the Three Level

Lead: ♠K

North
♠ 64
♡ 10
◇ AQJ1076
♣ A943

West
♠ KQJ9532
♡ Q9
◇ 532
♣ J

East
♠ 87
♡ K8432
◇ K4
♣ Q1065

South
♠ A10
♡ AJ765
◇ 98
♣ K872

West	North	East	South
—	—	Pass	1♡
3♠	Dbl	Pass	3NT
All Pass			

With the North hand, many would have responded 4◇ at their first turn, but our hero was a confirmed five-of-a-minor hater. He was careful to keep notrump in the picture. If partner could not bid 3NT, there was always time to show the diamonds later.

3NT proved to be no problem. Declarer ducked the spade lead and won the spade continuation. The diamond finesse lost to East, who could do no better than return a heart. South rose with the ♡A and took his nine tricks.

1♣ - (3♣) - Dbl

The 3♣ jump is natural, the same weak jump overcall it would be if partner had opened in another suit. Responder should have one or two majors and at least 10 HCP at this level to make a negative double.

Perfect double:

♠ A1064 ♡ KQ76 ◇ K632 ♣ 8
(Sometimes, life is easy. Anything partner does is okay.)

Imperfect double:

♠ 105432 ♡ A973 ◇ A954 ♣ —
(I am just not ready to bid 3♠ and force to game. Anything other than a negative double precludes finding a heart fit. I am also unwilling to risk 3♣ being passed out. My "lesser of evils" solution is the flexible negative double. If partner leaves it in, I do have two aces.)

Do not double with:

♠ KQ986 ♡ Q96543 ◇ 43 ♣ —
(Bid 4♣, Michaels-ish, showing at least 5-5 in the majors. Responder's cuebid normally promises a nice hand with support for opener's suit. However, this does not apply here because we cannot possibly want to play in clubs when RHO has at least six of them.)

Worth noting: if responder has a good hand, a club stopper and no four-card or longer major, he should be practical and bid 3NT, not 3◇, with a hand like this:

♠ J104 ♡ K3 ◇ AJ8654 ♣ K7

Opener Rebids after 1♣ - (3♣) - Dbl

Because the opponent's suit is also the suit you opened, this is quite a unique auction (along with 1◇ - (3◇) - Dbl). For the first time in our journey into opener's rebid, a penalty pass by opener becomes quite likely.

Pass with: ♠ 9743   ♡ AK   ◇ A53   ♣ QJ108
(This should be lucrative.)

Also pass with: ♠ AK   ♡ 942   ◇ 8754   ♣ KQ32
(Less obvious than the example above. Spot cards in the trump suit are often critical, but pass is still the percentage action here.)

Again, pass with: ♠ A98   ♡ A74   ◇ A63   ♣ 10864
(This could be wrong, but I would not get involved with a three-card suit at this level. Bidding would represent "scared bridge.")

Bid 3♡ with: ♠ 865   ♡ AQ97   ◇ K74   ♣ A43

3♠ with: ♠ 9875   ♡ AQ6   ◇ AJ10   ♣ J103
(Not enough clubs for a penalty pass, but enough spades to bid.)

4♣ with: ♠ AQ106   ♡ AQ97   ◇ A   ♣ 8542
(Cute, we are cuebidding our own suit, asking partner for his better major. That does not happen every day.)

4♡ with: ♠ AJ3   ♡ AKQ10   ◇ A62   ♣ J54
(Jumping with 100 honors and a lovely hand.)

4♠ with: ♠ KQJ9   ♡ KQ   ◇ AKJ   ♣ 7654

1◇ - (3♣) - Dbl

This double promises one or both majors and at least 10 HCP.

Perfect double:

♠ QJ43   ♡ K976   ◇ A1087   ♣ 5

Imperfect double:

♠ Q32   ♡ A973   ◇ AJ5   ♣ 743
(If opener responds 3♠, I will not be pleased. I will have no choice but to pass and apologize. No wonder I prefer to preempt the opponents before they can do it to me.)

Do not double with:

♠ K86543   ♡ J643   ◇ AK   ♣ K
(Bid 3♠. If partner bids 3NT, I would pass. If you double and opener rebids 3◇, you will not be well placed. Remember, a negative double followed by a bid in a new suit at the two or three level is not forcing.)

Major exception worth noting: a cardinal principle is that responder's raise of opener's minor denies a major. However, the auction 1◇ - (3♣) deserves special consideration. With hands like these, the correct bid is 3◇.

♠ A76   ♡ J652   ◇ Q9754   ♣ 8

♠ 10542   ♡ 98   ◇ AKJ4   ♣ 763

You are not strong enough to double even though you have a four-card major. If opener has a four-card major and a strong hand, he is welcome to bid it.

Opener Rebids after 1♦ - (3♣) - Dbl - (Pass)

✓ A cuebid is forcing to game.
✓ 3NT guarantees a stopper in the opponents suit.
✓ Opener may be forced to rebid a five-card suit.
✓ Opener should rarely introduce a three-card suit at the three level.

Pass with:　　　　　　♠ A3　♡ 84　♦ KQ98　♣ A7432
(An unexpected reward for opening 1♦.)

Bid 3♦ with:　　　　　♠ A42　♡ QJ　♦ AQ8543　♣ 98

3♡ with:　　　　　　　♠ KJ　♡ KQ87　♦ KJ85　♣ 765

3♠ with:　　　　　　　♠ AJ73　♡ A　♦ K5432　♣ 975

3NT with:　　　　　　♠ 96　♡ J43　♦ AKJ765　♣ AQ

4♣ with:　　　　　　　♠ K2　♡ AKJ　♦ AK7542　♣ 83
(Drive to game with this 18-point hand. If partner bids 4♡, you will settle there.)

4♦ with:　　　　　　　♠ 9　♡ KJ　♦ AKQJ876　♣ J32
(This is invitational. It sure would be nice if we had a way to ask partner for a club stopper.)

4♡ with:　　　　　　　♠ 9　♡ AK94　♦ AQ10854　♣ 87
(Too good for 3♡. If partner hates hearts, he can retreat to 5♦.)

4♠ with:　　　　　　　♠ AKJ8　♡ 763　♦ AQJ98　♣ 9

1♥ - (3♣) - Dbl

This negative double shows the unbid major along with the 10+ HCP needed at this level. If partner opens 1♠, the same concepts apply.

Perfect doubles:

♠ AQJ7 ♥ 87 ◇ K7543 ♣ 83

♠ KJ53 ♥ AJ ◇ A986 ♣ 742

Imperfect double:

♠ AKJ8 ♥ 10 ◇ J97543 ♣ 76
(Double. A compromise between the over-optimistic game-forcing 3◇ bid and the very pessimistic pass.)

Do not double with:

♠ AQ109 ♥ 854 ◇ K74 ♣ 743
(Bid a straightforward 3♥. Do not concern yourself with the possibility that a spade contract is better.)

♠ AJ1097 ♥ 63 ◇ K97654 ♣ —
(Bid 3♠ and insist on game. Do not double or bid 3◇. You are six-five and have a void in the opponent's suit, which is as good as having a king in your pocket. If partner responds 3NT, you should bid 4◇.)

Worth noting: responder must be practical at this level. Do not take a chance on making a trap pass with a hand like the following because partner will not always be able to reopen with a double. Bid 3NT with:

♠ QJ3 ♥ QJ ◇ J1074 ♣ AK92

Opener Rebids after 1♠ - (3♣) - Dbl - (Pass)

Pass with: ♠ KQ643 ♡ A ◇ A85 ♣ 10754
(Your alternatives are dubious, and you have excellent defense.
You must be prepared to occasionally end up -470.)

Bid 3◇ with: ♠ AQ764 ♡ J87 ◇ KQJ ♣ J2
(When in doubt, make the cheapest reasonable bid.)

3♡ with: ♠ K7432 ♡ K653 ◇ AQ ♣ 94

3♠ with: ♠ AK9732 ♡ KQ ◇ 85 ♣ 843
(Nice and easy, just the way I like it.)

Also bid 3♠ with: ♠ AKQJ9 ♡ K7 ◇ 754 ♣ 943
(It is rare to rebid a five-card suit at this level, but the strength of
this suit warrants it.)

3NT with: ♠ AQ732 ♡ 854 ◇ 942 ♣ AQ
(Minimum, schminimum. You have the requisite stopper, so bid
3NT like a champ.)

4♣ with: ♠ AJ743 ♡ AQ6 ◇ AJ83 ♣ 8

4◇ with: ♠ AQ1085 ♡ 8 ◇ AKJ43 ♣ 86
(Invitational to game in diamonds, or even spades.)

4♡ with: ♠ Q8543 ♡ AKQ10 ◇ A2 ♣ 83
(This hand is much too good for a 3♡ bid.)

4♠ with: ♠ AJ108543 ♡ 9 ◇ AKJ ♣ 84

Thrump Doubles

"Thrump doubles," as described here, were invented by yours truly. While they certainly are different, experience has shown that they are essential at the three level.

What is a thrump double and why do we need them? The discussion of the bidding on this hand will clue you in.

♠ Q7　♡ Q2　♢ 1087　♣ AKQJ75

Once your partner has opened the bidding, you are thinking about 3NT. In fact, I will bet that is the case regardless of which suit your partner opened. You will show your clubs and points and hope partner bids notrump sooner or later.

Nice plan. Now suppose that your RHO jumps to 3♢, 3♡ or 3♠ before you are able to make your first bid. Are you going to give up on the 3NT contract you were heading for? If you make the "normal" 4♣ bid, do you expect partner to provide the five tricks you will need to bring home 5♣?

What is my suggestion? Make a negative double. However, instead of defining it as looking for the unbid major(s), think of it as looking for **THR**ee notr**UMP**. On most hands where partner has a stopper in the opponent's suit, you would like him to bid 3NT.

When is this needed? When the enemy's natural jump overcall reaches 3♢, we cannot necessarily show our suit without going past 3NT. Here are the 10 auctions where the opponent has made a natural, preemptive jump overcall above 3♣ and below 3NT.

1♣ - (3♢)	1♣ - (3♡)	1♣ - (3♠)
1♢ - (3♢)	1♢ - (3♡)	1♢ - (3♠)
1♡ - (3♢)	1♠ - (3♡)	1♡ - (3♠)
1♠ - (3♢)		

Must you have a solid suit? Absolutely not. A thrump double would be totally appropriate after 1♡ - (3♠) with:

♠ 864 ♡ 65 ◇ AQ754 ♣ AQ2   or

♠ 93 ♡ K7 ◇ KQ10865 ♣ KQ8   or

♠ 63 ♡ A2 ◇ 852 ♣ AK10854

Now you are responder after 1♣ - (3♡).

♠ K3 ♡ 84 ◇ AKQJ5 ♣ J753
(Double, hoping partner bids 3NT.)

♠ KQ863 ♡ KQ2 ◇ K7 ♣ 985
(Forget your spades. You have hearts stopped so bid 3NT.)

♠ AK ♡ A64 ◇ AK83 ♣ J852
(Once in a blue moon you will have a great hand with a stopper in the opponent's suit. In that case, you can start with a negative double and then explore for slam.)

Thrump Double Summary

✓ **Applies when the jump overcall is 3◇, 3♡ or 3♠.**
✓ **Tells opener to bid 3NT when he has a stopper in the opponent's suit.**
✓ **Says nothing specific about responder's holding in the unbid suits.**
✓ **Almost always denies a stopper in the opponent's suit.**
✓ **Responder denies a five-card major that he could have bid at the three level.**
✓ **Promises at least 10 HCP and denies three-card support for opener's major.**

Worth noting: responder could have a very long minor.

1♣ - (3◇) - Dbl

Once the opponent's jump overcall reaches 3◇, we have a major development: no longer does responder's double promise any majors. 10 HCP is the minimum for this thrump double.

Perfect doubles:

♠ QJ4 ♡ Q107 ◇ J2 ♣ AKQ63

♠ AQ52 ♡ A974 ◇ 2 ♣ K1073

Imperfect double:

♠ 32 ♡ AQ63 ◇ 95 ♣ AQ743
(If partner bids clubs, hearts or notrump you will play game accordingly. If he bids 3♠, you will convert to clubs.)

Do not double with:

♠ 9854 ♡ KQ ◇ KJ6 ♣ KQ96
(Bid 3NT. Ignore your spades and acknowledge your two diamond stoppers.)

Worth noting: responder will sometimes need to choose between showing his major and bidding 3NT. Experience has shown that 3NT is usually the practical action. After 1♣ - (3◇), I would bid 3NT, not 3♠, with:

♠ KJ732 ♡ K65 ◇ AQ ♣ 643

Opener Rebids after 1♣ - (3◇) - Dbl - (Pass)

Pass with: ♠ AK ♡ Q4 ◇ 7542 ♣ A9743
(You have three quick tricks and your fourth diamond also argues
for defending.)

Bid 3♡ with: ♠ K6 ♡ KQ87 ◇ 84 ♣ KJ852

3♠ with: ♠ AJ95 ♡ 87 ◇ 854 ♣ AK83

3NT with: ♠ AQ ♡ 85 ◇ K75 ♣ A96543

Also bid 3NT with: ♠ KQJ10 ♡ J3 ◇ KQJ ♣ 9876
(You have beautiful spades. Sorry, after the opponents preempt,
notrump is number one.)

4♣ with: ♠ 8 ♡ A54 ◇ 974 ♣ AK9653

4◇ with: ♠ KQJ ♡ J765 ◇ 7 ♣ AKQ96
(You want to be in game, but you do not know where. You will
pass partner's bid of four of either major.)

4♡ with: ♠ 8 ♡ AK86 ◇ 97 ♣ AKJ1062

4♠ with: ♠ A1098 ♡ 87 ◇ A ♣ AJ7543

4NT with: ♠ 74 ♡ KQ9 ◇ A ♣ AKQ10542
(Blackwood. We are on our way to 6♣ or even seven. It would be
cowardly to worry about a club loser or spade problem.)

1♢ - (3♢) - Dbl

3♢ is a natural weak jump overcall—just like 1♣ - (3♣). However, the important tidbit we learned about 1♣ - (3♢) bears repeating here. Thrump doubles say nothing about the unbid majors. They show values, and this one denies a diamond stopper.

Perfect double:

   ♠ KJ64 ♡ AJ76 ♢ 7 ♣ K865

Imperfect doubles:

   ♠ K9 ♡ QJ ♢ 42 ♣ KQ76542
   (Double—looking for 3NT— makes more sense than bidding 4♣ en route to an 11-trick game.)

Do not double with:

   ♠ KJ109865 ♡ K743 ♢ — ♣ 87
   (I could almost write a book about this hand. The correct action is to bid 3♠, and then continue on to 4♠. This is the wrong time to look for a heart fit, not to mention that you do not want to risk a final contract of 3♢ doubled. Do not jump to 4♠, that would show a strong hand. Remember, "you cannot preempt a preempt." If you were tempted to pass because you have only seven HCP, you have "pointcountitis.")

Worth noting: after 1♢ - (3♢), responder's 4♢ bid would be Michaels and promise great length in both majors.

Opener Rebids after 1◇ - (3◇) - Dbl - (Pass)

Because LHO bid the suit you opened, this is a special auction.

Pass with: ♠ AK3 ♡ K ◇ KJ109 ♣ 98762
(We hope to make the opponents regret that they ever bid.)

Also pass with: ♠ 982 ♡ AK ◇ K6543 ♣ K53
(You would prefer to have better diamond spots, but you do have five of them.)

Again, pass with: ♠ A75 ♡ A83 ◇ 7432 ♣ AJ4
(You have a lot of defense and nowhere to go.)

Bid 3♡ with: ♠ Q64 ♡ KQJ3 ◇ 9632 ♣ AJ

3♠ with: ♠ KQ97 ♡ KJ ◇ 8653 ♣ A43

3NT with: ♠ 8543 ♡ 7542 ◇ AQJ ♣ AQ
(With only three diamonds, I am not ready to pass. Even if my major suits were not so dilapidated, I would bid 3NT with my two diamond stoppers. After all, partner did make a thrump double.)

4◇ with: ♠ AQJ7 ♡ AQ109 ◇ 432 ♣ KQ
(A lovely self-cuebid again. This is certainly more pleasing than the diamond suit we opened.)

4♡ with: ♠ AJ ♡ AKJ9 ◇ 8532 ♣ KQ5

4♠ with: ♠ AKQJ ♡ 98 ◇ A743 ♣ A52

1♠ - (3◇) - Dbl

This thrump double guarantees 10+ HCP, and denies both support for opener's major and a diamond stopper. Responder will often have length in clubs. The double says nothing about the unbid major. The concepts here are exactly the same if the opening bid had been 1♡.

Perfect double:

♠ AJ   ♡ KJ74   ◇ J2   ♣ K10974

Imperfect doubles:

♠ AK   ♡ 94   ◇ 8732   ♣ A8542
(I would like to have more hearts and fewer diamonds.)

♠ 73   ♡ A965   ◇ 7   ♣ A98643
(Only eight HCP, but I love the singleton, pair of aces and six-card suit.)

Do not double with:

♠ KJ   ♡ J742   ◇ KJ7   ♣ Q943
(Because of your diamond strength, 3NT is a lot more practical than a negative double.)

Worth noting: "support with support" is especially important on high-level auctions. After 1♠ - (3◇), bid 4♠, not 3♡, with:

♠ KJ8   ♡ AK875   ◇ 94   ♣ J64

Opener Rebids after 1♡ - (3◇) - Dbl - (Pass)

✓ A cuebid is forcing to game.
✓ 3NT guarantees a stopper in the opponent's suit.
✓ Opener may be forced to rebid a five-card suit.
✓ Opener should rarely introduce a three-card suit
   at the three level.

Pass with: ♠ AQ ♡ AK854 ◇ 7643 ♣ 94
(Holding 3½ quick tricks and four diamonds, I am happy to pass.)

Bid 3♠ with: ♠ KQ10 ♡ J8743 ◇ Q2 ♣ AJ9
(I looked real hard for an alternative, but there just wasn't one.)

3NT with: ♠ J72 ♡ K10732 ◇ A7 ♣ A82
(I have no idea where our nine tricks are coming from, but I am
following the thrump doubler's orders.)

4♣ with: ♠ A65 ♡ K7542 ◇ 4 ♣ KQ92
(No wise guy 3♠ bid for me.)

4◇ with: ♠ AJ ♡ A98543 ◇ 2 ♣ AQ103
(Yes, we have some slam interest, but our first priority is to find a
fit. If partner bids 4♠, I will bid 5♣.)

4♡ with: ♠ A9 ♡ KQJ976 ◇ 85 ♣ A107

4♠ with: ♠ KQ98 ♡ A8754 ◇ 9 ♣ KQ8
(If responder does not like spades, he will have a lot of clubs and
is welcome to bid them.)

5♣ with: ♠ 63 ♡ AK643 ◇ 7 ♣ KQ1095

1◇ - (3♡) - Dbl

Another thrump double. Responder should have at least 10 HCP, and will often have length in the unbid minor. He should not have a heart stopper (he would bid 3NT) or five spades (he would bid 3♠). Other than that, many spade holdings are possible. Nothing changes if the opening bid is 1♣.

Perfect double:

    ♠ KJ72 ♡ 86 ◇ A97 ♣ AJ65

Imperfect double:

    ♠ KQ8 ♡ 7 ◇ 932 ♣ A76543
(With a singleton in the opponent's suit, you cannot lose sleep about that missing 10th HCP.)

Do not double with:

    ♠ A864 ♡ K107 ◇ J654 ♣ AJ
(3NT is where it's at.)

    ♠ KQ1087 ♡ 7 ◇ A943 ♣ 976
(Bid 3♠. You had not planned on forcing to game, but it would be cowardly to pass. Nothing would be accomplished by suppressing your five-card major.)

Worth noting: responder should make a thrump double even with support for partner's minor in order to explore for 3NT. Therefore, after 1◇ - (3♡), I would double with this hand:

    ♠ K7 ♡ 532 ◇ KQJ75 ♣ QJ5

Opener Rebids after 1♣ - (3♡) - Dbl - (Pass)

Pass with: ♠ A ♡ 10854 ◇ AKQ ♣ 98432
(At this level, you need not wait for great trumps to penalty pass.)

Bid 3♠ with: ♠ AK98 ♡ J7 ◇ 94 ♣ A7543

3NT with: ♠ A65 ♡ K8 ◇ K63 ♣ K7543

Also bid 3NT with: ♠ AQJ ♡ KJ ◇ KQJ ♣ J7542
(Do not even consider a more aggressive bid. It is true that you have 18 HCP, but they are more *schmoints* than good cards. Jacks are quite overrated.)

4♣ with: ♠ 854 ♡ J7 ◇ AQ ♣ AQ8543
(This did not hurt at all.)

Also bid 4♣ with: ♠ QJ ♡ 643 ◇ KQJ ♣ KJ1072
(That hurt plenty.)

4◇ with: ♠ A7 ♡ 9 ◇ AKJ6 ♣ A87543
(Remember, opener's reverse from clubs to diamonds above the two level is forcing to game.)

4♡ with: ♠ AK8 ♡ 8 ◇ AKQ ♣ 1076532
(Where oh where is our fit? If partner bids 4♠, I will pass.)

4♠ with: ♠ AQ65 ♡ 87 ◇ A3 ♣ KQJ74

5♣ with   ♠ A6 ♡ 9 ◇ A109 ♣ AQ108765

1♠ - (3♡) - Dbl

Responder promises 10+ HCP, but denies both three cards in opener's major and a stopper in the opponent's suit. He has one or both minors.

Perfect doubles:

♠ K6   ♡ 53   ◇ AKJ9   ♣ Q9743

♠ AJ   ♡ J7   ◇ 976542   ♣ KQJ
(I am certainly not tempted to bid 4◇.)

Imperfect doubles:

♠ J9   ♡ 8   ◇ A8654   ♣ A10832
(You would not pass, would you?)

♠ J9   ♡ J6   ◇ J5   ♣ AKQJ732
(It is easier to take nine tricks in 3NT than 11 in 5♣.)

Do not double with:

♠ K8   ♡ —   ◇ A876   ♣ AQJ8654
(Bid 4♣. There is too much distribution and slam potential for you to double.)

Worth noting: thrump doubles will often get us to game, although they are definitely not game forcing. When responder doubles after 1♠ - (3♡) with a hand like this, he has done his all.

♠ 74   ♡ 852   ◇ K984   ♣ AK106

If opener can do nothing more interesting than bid 3♠ or four of a minor, responder should pass.

Opener Rebids after 1♠ - (3♡) - Dbl - (Pass)

Pass with: ♠ A8654   ♡ J87   ◇ AK   ♣ Q54
(You have a lot of defense—three quick tricks—and nothing to bid. Cross your fingers and hope for the best.)

Also pass with: ♠ 65432   ♡ 5432   ◇ AK   ♣ AQ

Bid 3♠ with: ♠ KQ1097   ♡ 95   ◇ A4   ♣ K963
(I would prefer to stay at the three level and rebid my chunky spades, rather than journey to the four level in a minor.)

3NT with: ♠ KJ1076   ♡ AK   ◇ J765   ♣ KJ

4♣ with: ♠ K8643   ♡ Q7   ◇ KQ   ♣ K1076
(An honest bid for an ugly hand.)

4◇ with: ♠ K6532   ♡ QJ   ◇ A8542   ♣ K

4♡ with: ♠ KQJ83   ♡ 9   ◇ AQ3   ♣ K843
(You have enough for game. Your singleton heart is huge.)

4♠ with: ♠ QJ108754   ♡ A2   ◇ AQ3   ♣ 8

5♣ with: ♠ A8543   ♡ —   ◇ 854   ♣ AKJ97
(Opener's jump to five of an unbid minor always promises a five-card suit. Your partner has denied heart values so all your high cards are well placed.)

1♣ - (3♠) - Dbl

For this thrump double, responder should have at least 10 HCP, and will often have length in the unbid minor. He should not have a spade stopper (he would bid 3NT) and definitely does not promise hearts. Nothing changes if the opening bid is 1◇.

Perfect double:

♠ 72   ♡ A863   ◇ KQ43   ♣ A87

Imperfect doubles:

♠ 984   ♡ A5   ◇ 932   ♣ AKJ43
(Yes, I really want you to double here. If partner does not bid 3NT, you will show your lovely club support.)

♠ 643   ♡ 94   ◇ AQJ952   ♣ A6
(If opener bids 4♡, you will correct to 5◇.)

Do not double with:

♠ 8   ♡ Q98743   ◇ A74   ♣ KJ5
(Bid 4♡. Thrump doubles were invented to avoid five-of-a-minor contracts. With a six-card major and reasonable values, bid your 10-trick game.)

Worth noting: responder can easily have five hearts to make a negative double after 1♣ - (3♠). He might have:

♠ 64   ♡ AJ532   ◇ A96   ♣ A74

Unilaterally bidding 4♡ with this hand would be frightening. If partner is short in hearts, this may become a hand that you will never forget.

Opener Rebids after 1 ◇ - (3♠) - Dbl - (Pass)

Pass with: ♠ J43   ♡ QJ7   ◇ KQJ6   ♣ KJ7
(Any bid you make would probably land you in hot water.)

Bid 3NT with: ♠ AJ4   ♡ J643   ◇ KQJ7   ♣ J8
(Partner's thrump double neither showed nor asked for hearts. Be thankful that you have a stopper and avoid over-thinking.)

4♣ with: ♠ 76   ♡ A4   ◇ A9865   ♣ KQ32

4◇ with: ♠ 7   ♡ AK7   ◇ KJ7532   ♣ J53

4♡ with: ♠ 8   ♡ AQ63   ◇ AJ865   ♣ J65
(If responder does not have hearts, he will pull to a minor.)

4♠ with: ♠ —   ♡ A42   ◇ AQ7643   ♣ K853
(Once partner has shown 10+ HCP and no wasted values in spades, your void becomes huge. You should always force to game with this type of hand and be thinking about slam.)

4NT with: ♠ 9   ♡ AKJ   ◇ AKJ86543   ♣ 7

5♣ with: ♠ 7   ♡ A3   ◇ KJ1065   ♣ KQ732

5◇ with: ♠ 9   ♡ A2   ◇ AK108654   ♣ Q63

1♡ - (3♠) - Dbl

This is the last of our thrump doubles. The requirements for this double are the same as for 1♠ - (3♡) - Dbl.

Perfect doubles:

   ♠ 87   ♡ AJ   ◇ A8754   ♣ KQ109

   ♠ 4   ♡ K7   ◇ A8743   ♣ A8642

Imperfect doubles:

   ♠ 8   ♡ 96   ◇ Q10843   ♣ AK1094
   (Passing is cowardly. The singleton spade is great and we like the minor-suit intermediates.)

   ♠ A74   ♡ A8   ◇ AQ96   ♣ A832
   (Partner will not know that you have a spade stopper, but your hand is much too good for 3NT. The flexible double is your best first move.)

Do not double with:

   ♠ A4   ♡ Q   ◇ KQJ653   ♣ J865
   (Honor thy stopper. Be practical and bid 3NT.)

   ♠ QJ98   ♡ —   ◇ KJ76   ♣ K7632
   (Trap pass. With more defense than offense, you hope to defend 3♠ doubled.)

Worth noting: responder should strive to double at the three-level, rather than bid four of a minor. The only exception is when his hand is either very strong or very distributional.

Opener Rebids after 1♡ - (3♠) - Dbl - (Pass)

Pass with: ♠ QJ107 ♡ AK876 ♢ K ♣ 843
(I expect to score more on defense than offense—even if we could make 3NT.)

Bid 3NT with: ♠ AQ ♡ Q10754 ♢ J ♣ KQJ109
(You have a nice club suit, but who cares. On thrump double auctions, experience has taught me to have a one-track mind.)

Also bid 3NT with: ♠ KQ10 ♡ AQJ862 ♢ 82 ♣ Q2
(Nine tricks look easier to take in notrump than ten in hearts.)

4♣ with: ♠ J74 ♡ KQJ76 ♢ 8 ♣ KQJ4

4♢ with: ♠ Q2 ♡ AK843 ♢ KJ83 ♣ 54

4♡ with: ♠ 92 ♡ AQ10854 ♢ 93 ♣ AQ7

4♠ with: ♠ — ♡ AQ432 ♢ A1087 ♣ A643
(Three aces and a void. That catches my eye. In fact, I intend to raise partner's minor to slam.)

5♢ with: ♠ — ♡ K8763 ♢ AK10983 ♣ 42
(Advocates of The Rule of 20 would not dream of passing initially. I have found that the best way to show a five-card major is to open it. Once partner shows some values: *points, schmoints,* you owe him a jump.)

Negative Doubles at Higher Levels

Negative Doubles at the Four Level

Finally, we made it to the four level. I would not have blamed you if you thought that our 3NT explorations would never end. With the notrump distraction behind us, we are free to concentrate on the classic decision—should we play or should we defend.

Defining a double as penalty is impractical at this level. After the auction has begun 1♣ - (4◇), the likelihood that responder will be dealt a hand like this is slim to none:

♠ A32   ♡ K765   ◇ AJ95   ♣ J7

Instead, he is far more likely to hold a hand like one of these:

♠ A965   ♡ KQJ3   ◇ K   ♣ 9543

♠ 108654   ♡ AQ95   ◇ 74   ♣ AQ

♠ A43   ♡ AJ109   ◇ 83   ♣ Q754

Not one of these typical hands is suitable for a penalty double. With each of them, responder must double and hope that partner does the right thing. I like opener's chances a lot better after a "general strength" negative double than after a penalty double.

Here is another Bergen recommendation, intended to make life bearable at the four level. With a void in the opponent's suit:

✓ Responder should not make a negative double.
✓ Opener should never pass a negative double.

What is the reason for this? Voids in the opponent's suit are terrible for defense (no trumps to ruff with) and great for offense (no losers).

Opener's Unique 4◇ Bid

The auction begins:

You	North	East	South
1 of a suit	4♣	Dbl	Pass
?			

The spotlight is on opener. With a balanced hand, he simply passes. If he makes a bid, the partnership will almost always be in game. The only exception is when that bid is 4◇.

It is extremely unlikely that stopping on a dime in 4◇ will be best. Therefore, **after a negative double of 4♣, opener's 4◇ bid is forcing**. Opener may have diamonds, but he will often be hoping to play in four of a major. This waiting bid will allow opener to stall with a tough hand.

For example, you open 1♠ and the auction continues:

1♠ - (4♣) - Dbl - (Pass)

What would you bid with the following hands?

♠ Q87543   ♡ KQJ   ◇ AJ43   ♣ —

♠ KQ1043   ♡ AQ4   ◇ Q8432   ♣ —

♠ KQJ63   ♡ AJ10   ◇ KQ76   ♣ 5

These are the types of problems that would cause experts to lose sleep. On each of them, you:

✔ Are unwilling to pass,
✔ Want to be in game (at least),
✔ Have no idea where you want to play the hand.

Rather than guess, I would bid 4◇, forcing. No guarantees, but I like our chances a lot better once we allow partner to contribute to the decision-making process.

1♦ - (4♣) - Dbl

Responder is promising at least 10 HCP, just as he did at the three level. While responder does not guarantee both majors, he is quite likely to have at least one.

The auction 1♣ - (4♣) is far from impossible. I would be delighted to jump to 4♣ after my RHO opened 1♣ with:

♠ — ♡ 6 ♦ 9754 ♣ KQJ109653

Anyway, for the hands below, you are responding after the auction 1♦ - (4♣).

Perfect double:

♠ A965 ♡ AQ87 ♦ J64 ♣ 85

Imperfect double:

♠ KJ ♡ A9752 ♦ A942 ♣ 73
(We would need longer or better hearts to bid 4♡. If opener bids 4♠, we will bid 5♦.)

Do not double with:

♠ Q752 ♡ J97543 ♦ AK6 ♣ —
(Bid 4♡. Your suit is not great, but you do have six of them.)

Worth noting: just as 1♦ - (3♣) - 3♦ did not deny a major, a raise to 4♦ here would not deny one either. 4♦ is a standout with a hand like this:

♠ A76 ♡ 10765 ♦ J97543 ♣ —

If opener continues by bidding four of a major, it should be natural and is not forcing.

Opener Rebids after 1◇ - (4♣) - Dbl - (Pass)

✓ 4◇ is forcing.
✓ Never pass with a void in the opponent's suit.
✓ Do not rebid a five-card suit.
✓ Do not introduce a three-card suit.

Pass with: ♠ A65 ♡ KQ ◇ K8754 ♣ 732
(With a balanced hand, you should pass without thought.)

Bid 4◇ with: ♠ AQ107 ♡ J643 ◇ AJ109 ♣ 9
(I defined this as forcing to game. It is very nice not to have to choose a major all by myself.)

Also bid 4◇ with: ♠ K9 ♡ AKJ9 ◇ AQ8754 ♣ 9
(We are very interested in slam but need partner's input.)

4♡ with: ♠ K54 ♡ AQ96 ◇ K7643 ♣ 5

4♠ with: ♠ KQJ7 ♡ 83 ◇ KQJ64 ♣ 53

4NT with: ♠ 8 ♡ AKQ3 ◇ KQJ7543 ♣ 8

5♣ with: ♠ AQ32 ♡ AJ54 ◇ KQ1085 ♣ —
(A cuebid at the five level promises a void and is forcing to slam.)

5◇ with: ♠ Q76 ♡ KQ ◇ KQJ10876 ♣ 9

1♡ - (4♣) - Dbl

This negative double will usually promise the unbid major. It will also deny a club void. If responder has a great diamond suit, he should bid 4◇ rather than double. If the opening bid is 1♠, these concepts apply.

Perfect double:

♠ AQ76   ♡ AQ   ◇ 97643   ♣ 98

Imperfect double:

♠ Q754   ♡ A   ◇ KQ976   ♣ 765
(I would be happier if the ♣5 were the ♡5.)

Do not double with:

♠ J9765   ♡ KJ   ◇ KQ9743   ♣ —
(Bid 4◇. A double is too likely to be left in. This hand is screaming offense, not defense.)

♠ AKJ7   ♡ 432   ◇ KQ9   ♣ 743
(Bid 4♡. Simple is best.)

Worth noting: if opener bids 4◇, responder should take a preference to 4♡ with a doubleton. Remember, he has already denied three-card support for opener's major.

Opener Rebids after 1♠ - (4♣) - Dbl - (Pass)

Pass with: ♠ A7654 ♡ KJ7 ◇ AJ ♣ 954

Bid 4◇ with: ♠ AKJ76 ♡ KJ8 ◇ A965 ♣ 8
(Remember, after responder's negative double of 4♣, opener's 4◇
bid is 100% forcing to game.)

Also bid 4◇ with: ♠ AQ8543 ♡ 64 ◇ AK65 ♣ 7
(This does not preclude playing in 4♠.)

4♡ with: ♠ KQ1076 ♡ KQJ9 ◇ K8 ♣ 97

4♠ with: ♠ QJ10985 ♡ KQJ ◇ QJ ♣ J3
(I doubt we can make this, but it is the normal action after
partner's non-penalty double. You do not want to defend because
you might contribute no tricks against 4♣ doubled.)

5♣ with: ♠ A7643 ♡ AK87 ◇ KJ103 ♣ —
(I am on my way to slam in diamonds or hearts.)

5◇ with: ♠ K6543 ♡ K9 ◇ KQJ75 ♣ 4

5♠ with: ♠ AKJ97653 ♡ Q63 ◇ K7 ♣ —
(This bid invites a spade slam. Partner should know to upgrade his
honors outside clubs when making this decision.)

1♣ - (4♢) - Dbl

This negative double promises at least 10 HCP and denies a void in diamonds. Although it does not guarantee both majors, responder usually has at least one (which can be five cards long.)

Perfect double:

♠ K1076　♡ AK87　♢ 8　♣ J965

Imperfect doubles:

♠ A7　♡ KQ75　♢ 643　♣ K765
(If opener bids 4♠, you will bid 5♣.)

♠ 96532　♡ 86543　♢ A　♣ AQ
(It is likely that you belong in game in partner's better major, but there is no single bid that will allow you to find it. Four "sparts" anyone?)

Do not double with:

♠ AQJ6　♡ Q3　♢ 9　♣ J98532
(Bid 5♣. Support with support.)

Worth noting: responder will rarely be confident when he introduces his major after 1♣ - (4♢) - ? Therefore, opener should bid whenever he is void in the opponent's suit. After the auction begins 1♣ - (4♢) - 4♡ - (Pass), opener should bid 4♠ holding:

♠ K1094　♡ —　♢ KJ7　♣ A97654

Opener Rebids after 1♣ - (4◇) - Dbl - (Pass)

Pass with: ♠ AK ♡ J654 ◇ QJ9 ♣ K754
(This is much better than bidding 4♡. Even if partner does have four hearts, a bad split is likely. Take your sure plus.)

Bid 4♡ with: ♠ 72 ♡ AQ87 ◇ 6 ♣ AQ7543
(My kind of shape.)

4♠ with: ♠ KJ107 ♡ J62 ◇ 9 ♣ AK632

Also bid 4♠ with: ♠ AKJ9 ♡ J742 ◇ — ♣ KJ853
(I wish that I had a waiting bid available in order to bring hearts into the picture. I will bid my better major with this hand. If my major-suit holdings were close in strength, I would respond 4♡, bidding up the line.)

4NT with: ♠ A ♡ AK9 ◇ 4 ♣ KQJ97543
(A club slam is looking good.)

5♣ with: ♠ A64 ♡ A53 ◇ — ♣ K976432
(I sure hope that partner has some clubs.)

5◇ with: ♠ QJ74 ♡ A1065 ◇ — ♣ AKQ53

5♡ with: ♠ K65 ♡ AQJ6 ◇ — ♣ A109543
(Invitational. With the gorgeous diamond void, you are too good to settle for 4♡.)

1♠ - (4◇) - Dbl

This auction may appear to be very similar to 1♠ - (4♣) - Dbl, but appearances are deceiving. After the enemy 4♣ overcall, responder had the ability to show a long diamond suit while remaining at the four level. With that option removed, overcoming the preempt is even more difficult.

This negative double promises 10 HCP but does not guarantee four hearts. If opener starts with 1♡, similar principles apply.

Perfect double:

♠ K7 ♡ KJ85 ◇ 73 ♣ AJ754

Imperfect doubles:

♠ 87 ♡ AJ107 ◇ 9 ♣ A97542
(With great shape, the 10 HCP requirement can be shaded. That is especially true when you have two aces.)

♠ J10 ♡ Q74 ◇ A6 ♣ K97653
(If opener bids 4♡, you are not well placed. I would take a preference to 4♠, which will work out well unless partner is specifically 5-5 in the majors.)

Do not double with:

♠ 7 ♡ KJ105 ◇ 8 ♣ KQJ9765
(Bid 5♣. Sometimes, a natural bid is best.)

Worth noting: because responder would have to bid 5♣ to introduce that suit on this auction, he will often make a negative double with a lot of clubs.

Opener Rebids after 1♡ - (4◇) - Dbl - (Pass)

Pass with: ♠ KQ ♡ KJ763 ◇ 943 ♣ QJ10
(If opener has a balanced hand at this level, he should pass.)

Bid 4♡ with: ♠ K7 ♡ KJ9532 ◇ 7 ♣ KQ109
(If partner has one heart and five or six clubs, I will feel stupid, not for the first or last time. However, I am not venturing to the five level in a four-card minor when I have a six-card major.)

Also bid 4♡ with: ♠ 9543 ♡ AKJ984 ◇ 2 ♣ KJ
(Rebidding hearts seems more prudent than speculating with these ratty spades.)

Bid 4♠ with: ♠ AKQ9 ♡ K96542 ◇ Q7 ♣ 6
(With this 6-4 hand, I will take my chances on the stronger suit.)

Also bid 4♠ with: ♠ AQ97 ♡ AQ543 ◇ 9 ♣ J107

4NT with: ♠ A ♡ KQJ10876 ◇ 5 ♣ KQ97
(There is virtually no chance that partner is aceless.)

5♣ with: ♠ 1087 ♡ A9765 ◇ — ♣ KQJ98
(The Rule of 20 enabled you to open 1♡. Now you will tell partner about your clubs. If you had passed initially and RHO had opened 4◇, you and partner would be in the dark.)

5◇ with: ♠ AJ54 ♡ AQ974 ◇ — ♣ KQ95
(This bid promises a diamond void and is forcing to slam.)

5♡ with: ♠ A85 ♡ AKQJ752 ◇ — ♣ 942
(We are making a general slam try with great hearts.)

4NT Takeout after a Four of a Major Overcall

We are now ready to discuss what to do when an opponent overcalls 4♡ or 4♠. Because the overcall is a game contract, it might be based on a good hand.

Regardless of the strength of his hand, **when a player makes a jump overcall to four of a major, he is eager to declare**. At the risk of stating the obvious, if something is advantageous for your opponents, it cannot be good for you.

This is all fine and good, but after responder's four-level negative double, it will be difficult for opener to find a suit to bid when he has a balanced hand. Responder must help him out. Responder can and should make a negative double with a fairly balanced hand. However, when he has incredible shape he should not double, he should bid and take the pressure off opener.

When responder has two long suits (other than spades), 4NT takeout is just what the doctor ordered. I will begin with a very shapely example.

You are delighted to pick up:

♠ 65 ♡ — ◇ Q76532 ♣ KQJ107

You probably cannot even remember the last time you were dealt a six-five hand. Partner opens 1♠ and your RHO jumps to 4♡. You do not know who can make what, but you have no intention of defending 4♡. Voids in the opponent's trump suit cry out for offense.

Unfortunately, you have no idea which minor should be trump. However, if you allow partner to make the decision, you should get to the optimum contract. **Bid 4NT—a variation of the unusual notrump—asking partner to bid his longer/better minor**.

When the overcall is 4♡, responder's 4NT bid always shows the minors. If he is two-suited with spades and a minor, he bids 4♠. For instance, after 1♣ - (4♡), I would bid 4♠ with:

♠ KQ1086   ♡ 4   ◇ K86432   ♣ 7

When the overcall is 4♠, hearts are very much in the picture. After 1♣ - (4♠), I would happily bid 4NT, showing hearts and a minor, with:

♠ —   ♡ Q86543   ◇ AJ965   ♣ 86
(Six-five distribution is ideal for this bid.)

After 1◇- (4♠) holding:

♠ —   ♡ QJ1087   ◇ 865   ♣ KJ942
(Bid 4NT. We are not six-five, but we do have a void.)

As these examples illustrate, 4NT does not promise a good hand. It might lead to a sacrifice against the enemy's game.

4NT is always unusual after any jump overcall of 4♡ or 4♠. The following chart will help you remember which specific suits are shown by this bid.

Auction	Responder's 4NT Shows
1♣ - (4♡)	minors
1◇ - (4♡)	minors
1♠ - (4♡)	minors
1♣ - (4♠)	diamonds and hearts
1◇ - (4♠)	clubs and hearts
1♡ - (4♠)	minors

1♣ - (4♡) - Dbl

This double is negative, promises 10 points and denies a heart void. However, it is impractical for it to guarantee spades. Nothing changes if the opening bid is 1♢.

Perfect doubles:

♠ A754 ♡ 7 ♢ A9763 ♣ A54

♠ KQ107 ♡ 85 ♢ A762 ♣ Q96

Imperfect doubles:

♠ AJ6 ♡ A ♢ Q86543 ♣ 943
(If partner bids 4♠, you will pass and cross your fingers.)

♠ AQ ♡ 43 ♢ AQ754 ♣ J1043
(A negative double is your best action. If opener bids 4♠, you will bid 5♣.)

Do not double with:

♠ KQ876 ♡ 8 ♢ KQ875 ♣ 63
(Bid 4♠ and hope to find a suitable dummy. I do not know about you, but I am getting tired of preempts.)

Worth noting: if responder bids 4NT, it is takeout for the minors. He will typically have four-card support for opener's suit and six cards in the unbid minor. After 1♣ - (4♡), responder should bid 4NT with this hand:

♠ 52 ♡ 8 ♢ AQ10872 ♣ KJ73

Opener Rebids after 1♦ - (4♡) - Dbl - (Pass)

✓ Never pass with a void in the opponent's suit.
✓ Do not rebid a five-card suit
✓ Do not introduce a three-card suit.

Pass with: ♠ A83 ♡ AJ ♦ J7643 ♣ K87

Also pass with: ♠ 532 ♡ J5 ♦ KQJ7 ♣ KQJ3
(I do not like it, but I cannot even dream of bidding.)

Bid 4♠ with: ♠ J1095 ♡ J4 ♦ KQJ96 ♣ KQ
(When in doubt, bid 4♠ over 4♡.)

Also bid 4♠ with: ♠ AKJ9 ♡ 9 ♦ Q87432 ♣ K8
(With this shape, we have no doubts.)

4NT with: ♠ A72 ♡ — ♦ AJ7432 ♣ KJ74
(**4NT is also takeout by opener.** We are not sure whether we want to play 5♣ or 5♦.)

5♣ with: ♠ 76 ♡ 9 ♦ KQ843 ♣ AQJ106

5♦ with: ♠ A8 ♡ 8 ♦ KQ98654 ♣ QJ10

Also bid 5♦ with: ♠ K75 ♡ 4 ♦ KQ10976 ♣ KJ9
(An extra diamond would be nice. Interesting, that is exactly what my wife has been telling me.)

5♡ with: ♠ AQ65 ♡ — ♦ AQ953 ♣ AJ108
(We are on our way to slam in whatever suit partner prefers.)

1♠ - (4♡) - Dbl

This negative double denies three spades, while promising at least 10 HCP. It can include a long minor suit that is not worth bidding at the five level. As with all four-level negative doubles, responder should never have a void in the opponent's suit.

Perfect double:

♠ A6 ♡ 86 ◇ Q8743 ♣ AQ52

Imperfect double:

♠ KJ ♡ A ◇ Q7643 ♣ J8432
(You have more offense and less defense than you might like, but bidding 4NT with such bad suits would be over-reacting.)

Do not double with:

♠ 432 ♡ J7 ◇ AQ104 ♣ KJ54
(Bid 4♠. Support with support.)

♠ 7 ♡ 8 ◇ KQJ98 ♣ KQ8543
(Bid 4NT, unusual. You are likely to have a good fit for partner's better minor.)

Worth noting: The Law of Total Tricks demonstrates that it is important to try to bid 4♠ over 4♡ whenever humanly possible. Therefore, responder can make this bid with some very weak hands. Bid 4♠ at any vulnerability with:

♠ Q7652 ♡ 8 ◇ 97 ♣ 86532

Of course, I would also bid 4♠ with:

♠ KQJ6 ♡ K82 ◇ KQJ ♣ J74

That is why people preempt.

Opener Rebids after 1♠ - (4♡) - Dbl - (Pass)

Pass with: ♠ KQ854 ♡ A4 ◇ A86 ♣ 954

Bid 4♠ with: ♠ AJ9865 ♡ — ◇ KQ7 ♣ 9654
(These spades are not great, but with six of them and a heart void,
I would not pass.)

4NT with: ♠ K9653 ♡ — ◇ AJ74 ♣ AJ74
(4NT is always takeout after a four-of-a-major jump overcall. We
must have exactly 4-4 in the minors for this bid. In fact, partner
knows our entire shape after our 1♠ opening bid. What a great
convention! I cannot imagine how even less experienced players
could survive without this. Now that partner knows about our heart
void, all he needs to jump to slam is a long minor.)

5♣ with: ♠ A9643 ♡ 9 ◇ K7 ♣ KQ1096

5◇ with: ♠ KQ976 ♡ 4 ◇ AQJ65 ♣ 43

5♠ with: ♠ AKJ10543 ♡ 9 ◇ AQ95 ♣ 8
(There is no realistic way to investigate a diamond slam, so stick
to your superb spades.)

1◇ - (4♠) - Dbl

This double promises at least 10 HCP and denies a spade void. Responder does not promise hearts. The meaning of the double is unchanged if partner opens 1♣.

Perfect double:

    ♠ 84 ♡ AQ65 ◇ K74 ♣ A942

Imperfect doubles:

    ♠ 7 ♡ KQJ5 ◇ 962 ♣ KQ643
(Without any aces, our defensive prospects are dubious. We are rooting for partner to bid.)

    ♠ AJ4 ♡ AQ5 ◇ 843 ♣ 8532
(Now we are rooting for partner to pass.)

Do not double with:

    ♠ 7 ♡ KQ874 ◇ KQJ4 ♣ 652
(Bid 5◇. This hand has great support for diamonds and more offense than defense.)

    ♠ 8 ♡ KJ1053 ◇ A ♣ J96432
(Bid 4NT, which shows the two unbid suits on this auction. With six-five, you want your side to declare.)

    ♠ — ♡ AQ10942 ◇ 852 ♣ KQ86
(Bid 5♡. Any partner worth his salt will have some heart support for you.)

Worth noting: with a void in the overcaller's suit, opener should not pass responder's double.

Opener Rebids after 1♣ - (4♠) - Dbl - (Pass)

Pass with: ♠ A6 ♡ KQ ♢ J754 ♣ Q10974

Also pass with: ♠ Q ♡ A874 ♢ AQ8 ♣ J7543
(You do not have enough shape to bid at the five level.)

Bid 4NT with: ♠ — ♡ AQ85 ♢ 8765 ♣ KQJ98

5♣ with: ♠ 8 ♡ KJ104 ♢ J ♣ AQJ10765
(Do not even think about bidding hearts.)

Also bid 5♣ with: ♠ 9 ♡ AQ ♢ K74 ♣ QJ109643

5♢ with: ♠ — ♡ 76 ♢ AKJ84 ♣ AQ7643
(The reverse at the five level shows an exceptional hand.)

Also bid 5♢ with: ♠ — ♡ K7 ♢ A8743 ♣ AK8743

5♡ with: ♠ 9 ♡ AKQ9 ♢ K7 ♣ A87642
(Because partner did not promise hearts, you should have great
hearts and a very strong unbalanced hand for this bid.)

5♠ with: ♠ — ♡ AJ76 ♢ K876 ♣ AKJ109

1♡ - (4♠) - Dbl

For the first time, we have an auction where responder can double with support for opener's major. You should not bid 5♡ on this auction with:

♠ K5   ♡ 643   ◇ A865   ♣ A842.

Other than that, we have our typical four-level scenario. Responder cannot have a spade void for this double, and promises at least 10 HCP.

Perfect doubles:

♠ AJ   ♡ K7   ◇ A7542   ♣ J853

♠ 752   ♡ A9   ◇ AQJ   ♣ 97432

Imperfect double:

♠ 1096   ♡ K64   ◇ KQ72   ♣ A54
(With a balanced hand, responder should never venture to the five level.)

Do not double with:

♠ —   ♡ A9   ◇ K76432   ♣ K9832
(Bid 4NT as takeout for the minors.)

♠ 8   ♡ KQ87   ◇ KQJ43   ♣ 943
(Bid 5♡. It is annoying when their suit outranks yours.)

Worth noting: once we define 4NT as takeout, we are out of luck when responder is dealt the very rare hand that was suitable for Blackwood. After 1♡ - (4♠), I would bid 6◇ with:

♠ 8   ♡ 6   ◇ AKQ97654   ♣ AK3

Opener Rebids after 1♡ - (4♠) - Dbl - (Pass)

Pass with: ♠ K7   ♡ AJ754   ◇ J743   ♣ A2

Also pass with: ♠ 8   ♡ AKJ64   ◇ J543   ♣ KJ6
(I do not like to pass with a singleton trump, but there is nowhere to go with this hand.)

Bid 4NT with: ♠ —   ♡ K8543   ◇ KJ74   ♣ KQ32

5♣ with: ♠ 8   ♡ QJ875   ◇ 2   ♣ AKJ543
(You opened this great distributional hand 1♡. Now bid your second suit and avoid defending.)

Also bid 5♣ with: ♠ —   ♡ J86532   ◇ 965   ♣ AKQJ
(I would like to have a fifth club, but these four are pretty nice. I have learned not to defend with a trump void on these auctions.)

5◇ with: ♠ 8   ♡ A7643   ◇ KQ972   ♣ A2

Also bid 5◇ with: ♠ —   ♡ KQJ85   ◇ 85432   ♣ KQJ
(These diamonds may not be worth showing off, but you do have 24-carat distribution.)

5♡ with: ♠ 8   ♡ KQJ8654   ◇ AJ98   ♣ 9

5♠ with: ♠ —   ♡ AK765   ◇ AKQ   ♣ 98543
(We are on our way to slam—partner will guide us.)

1 Suit - (5 Minor) - Dbl

When I suggest that a double is still negative here, I am only saying that responder will not have a trump stack. In addition, he could easily have support for opener's suit when he doubles.

Alert: the auction for this page is 1♡ - (5◇).

Perfect doubles:

♠ AQJ7 ♡ K7 ◇ 73 ♣ Q10854

♠ K84 ♡ A9 ◇ K72 ♣ K7532

Imperfect double:

♠ K9762 ♡ K7 ◇ 8 ♣ A8532
(Your hand is unbalanced, but you have no suit worth bidding at this level.)

Do not double with:

♠ 9743 ♡ AQJ ◇ — ♣ KJ7643
(Bid 5♡, even though you would like to have another heart.)

♠ KQ10985 ♡ 9 ◇ 4 ♣ KQJ54
(Bid 5♠.)

Worth noting: opener will only pull responder's double of five of a minor about 15% of the time.

Opener Rebids after 1♠ - (5♣) - Dbl - (Pass)

Pass with: ♠ AQ8654 ♡ AJ7 ◇ 976 ♣ 3
(Do not even think about bidding. In general, **unless you have
incredible distribution, the five level belongs to the opponents**.)

Also pass with: ♠ Q9765 ♡ KQ ◇ AKQ6 ♣ 54
(You have a nice hand and beautiful diamonds, but not enough
shape to justify bidding.)

Bid 5◇ with: ♠ KQJ98 ♡ 865 ◇ KQJ65 ♣ —
(With so much offense, and very little defense, it would be
criminal to suppress your second suit. I'm a bidder.)

5♡ with: ♠ J87543 ♡ AKQJ9 ◇ 9 ♣ 6

5♠ with: ♠ KQ108754 ♡ KJ7 ◇ Q84 ♣ —

Also bid 5♠ with: ♠ KQJ1097 ♡ 85 ◇ A8653 ♣ —
(With spades like these, do not speculate on the value of your
diamonds.)

5NT with: ♠ AQ8765 ♡ AQ7 ◇ K852 ♣ —
(This bid shows a slam-going hand, but not a true three-suiter.)

6♣ with: ♠ K8654 ♡ AQ76 ◇ AQ109 ♣ —
(Here is your three-suited hand.)

6◇ with: ♠ AJ7654 ♡ 8 ◇ AK8743 ♣ —

Preserving all Options

Lead: ♣8

North
♠ K543
♡ K9
◇ 6
♣ A107643

West
♠ J97
♡ Q
◇ KQ1097543
♣ 8

East
♠ AQ106
♡ 432
◇ 8
♣ KJ952

South
♠ 82
♡ AJ108765
◇ AJ2
♣ Q

West	North	East	South
—	—	—	1♡
4◇	Dbl	Pass	4♡
All pass			

North was delighted to make a negative double after West's annoying preempt. South's 4♡ rebid was painless.

West's club lead had all the earmarks of a singleton. It was also likely that East had only one diamond. Therefore, declarer was afraid that either opponent would overruff a minor and return a trump. He won the ♣A and led the ◇6 to his ace. He now found the line of play which insured his contract. He ruffed a diamond with dummy's ♡K and then led a club and ruffed it with his ♡A.

Declarer was now able to ruff his last diamond with dummy's ♡9. The opposition could take the ♡Q at their leisure, but the contract was assured, losing just two spades and one trump.

Advanced Treatments

Responder's Three-Card Suits

As we have seen, responder is often in a quandary after the enemy overcalls. These annoying hands are good examples.

After 1◇ - (1♠) - ? what would you do with:

♠ 854   ♡ KQJ   ◇ 765   ♣ K642   or

♠ 854   ♡ 765   ◇ AKQ   ♣ 8642

Obviously, these two hands have a lot in common. For each, here are your choices:

Pass: certainly does not tell your partner about your values.
Negative double: you only have three hearts.
1NT: a blatant lie about your spade holding.
2♣: you lack the 10 HCP needed for this forward-going bid.
2◇: you need four cards in opener's suit to raise his minor.

Take a look at the first example. With no good bid available, many players would pass. I do not agree. I would make a negative double, thinking that ♡ KQJ is not so different than ♡ 5432. Playing a 4-3 fit at the two level when I hold KQJ is not a problem.

On the second example, I would also prefer not to pass. This time I will take note of my 14-carat diamonds and raise to 2◇. The 4-3 fit still does not bother me. Could partner have opened 1◇ with only three diamonds? Possible but highly unlikely.

Length is more important than strength. However, it is also true, that **the strength of our suits is often critical**. As I once remarked when a student asked, "How many cards does opener need to raise responder's major," "I have four, except when I have three good ones."

Responder's Jump Cuebid as a Transfer to 3NT

As I wrote in *More Points Schmoints*, the key to who should become declarer is not overall strength. Very often, one player will have a holding he needs to "protect." In that case, it is in our best interest that he declare.

For example, if one player holds Qx in a suit, and his partner holds Axx, we desperately want the hand with the Qx to declare. Now, regardless of which opponent holds the king, we are assured of eventually winning two tricks if this suit is led by the opponents.

The above is especially relevant after an opponent overcalls. It is definitely in our best interest to put him on lead because he will be leading away from strength. Voilà. When RHO has overcalled, our jump cuebid has allowed opener to declare 3NT.

Case in point. Partner opens 1♣ and RHO overcalls 1♠. **Responder's jump cuebid of 3♠ denies four hearts and shows an opening bid with at least one spade stopper.** We expect that opener will bid 3NT unless he has a very strong or very unbalanced hand which is unsuitable for that contract. Opener's spade holding is irrelevant, but notice the bonus when responder has Axx and opener has Qx (as above). The potential "bonus combinations" are infinite, but you never lose when the overcaller is on lead.

I have used this bid for many years with no bad results and many good ones. A rival expert even went so far as to say that this is the best convention I have ever invented. I don't know about that, but it was certainly critical on the following deal.

North
♠ KJ
♡ J1063
◇ KQJ9
♣ K74

West
♠ 74
♡ 842
◇ 8765
♣ QJ92

East
♠ Q109853
♡ A75
◇ A4
♣ 83

South
♠ A62
♡ KQ9
◇ 1032
♣ A1065

It is easy to develop nine tricks in 3NT with any lead other than a spade from West. With North as declarer, the ♠J is protected and the contract rolls home.

At the other table, my opponents bid:

West	North	East	South
—	1◇	1♠	3NT
All pass			

West led the ♠7. Down two.

At our table, we bid:

West	North	East	South
—	1◇	1♠	3♠*
Pass	3NT	All pass	

(3♠* alerted as a transfer to 3NT)

East led the ♠10. Making five.

One Time Only —You Can "Preempt a Preempt"

Most players know that "you can't preempt a preempt." Accordingly, after an opponent's weak jump overcall, a jump shift by responder shows a strong hand (17+ HCP) rather than a weak jump shift such as this:

♠ KJ109862   ♡ 972   ◇ 76   ♣ 5

Of course, once partner has opened, the idea of passing with this lovely long suit bothers me tremendously. Unfortunately, the hand is not strong enough for a 2♠ bid, which would show at least 10 HCP. Responder would have to pass, what a waste.

The upshot of the above is that some partnerships have agreed that **after a weak jump overcall, responder's jump shift to the three level should be weak, not strong**. For this unique scenario, we can "preempt a preempt."

This seems to allow the best of both worlds. With a very strong hand such as this:

♠ AK10874   ♡ A76   ◇ 83   ♣ AQ

I prefer to bid only 2♠ after 1♣ - (2◇). Remember, a new suit by responder is forcing and unlimited. With a big hand, you prefer to keep the bidding low, which allows more room to exchange information and explore for your best contract.

If your partnership can handle an isolated exception like this, it strikes me as a very sensible agreement.

Alternative Lifestyle

Most of what we have discussed regarding negative doubles represents generally-accepted practice. We will now explore a few modern alternatives.

Four-Four or Four-Three?

In standard bridge, a negative double after 1♣ - (1♢) promises at least 4-4 in the majors. However, some experts play the following: a negative double can also be made with 4-3 in the majors, but only if the three-card major is very strong and the four-card suit is weak.

After 1♣ - (1♢), these players would double instead of responding 1♠ holding:

♠ 8654   ♡ AQ10   ♢ 743   ♣ K72

Bidding 1♠ would create the possibility of playing in a 4-3 "fit", which is awful with these deplorable spades. If partner bids hearts, our three honors will more than suffice.

I can personally vouch for the fact that Larry Cohen and I played this style for many years, and were quite happy with it.

1 Minor - (1♡) - 1♠ with Just Four?

After 1 of a minor - (1♡), common practice dictates that responder should double with four spades and bid 1♠ with five of them. I agree. However, there are two dissenting factions.

One group advocates bidding a strong four-card spade suit. They would respond 1♠ with holdings such as AJ107, KQJ4 and AK109. Opener is welcome to raise with three-card support just as he would if responder had promised five.

There is another group of players who are very concerned about the following dilemma. How would you feel with these hands after your partner opened 1♣ and your RHO overcalled 1♡?

♠ K3   ♡ 653   ◇ KQ543   ♣ J62

♠ 854   ♡ J4   ◇ AKJ74   ♣ 952

Personally, I would wish to be elsewhere. You would like to take some action once partner opened, but have no reasonable bid. Our second faction has no problem in this situation. They would make a negative double, their partners would alert and when asked explain "the double denies spades."[1]

The corollary to this treatment is: whenever responder has four or more spades he responds 1♠, exactly as he would if there had been no overcall.

While most of us are content with our regular treatment of this auction (double shows four, 1♠ shows at least five), it is easy to see the merits of both groups of dissenters.

---

[1]Although negative doubles are no longer "alertable" in duplicate bridge, any special understandings should be alerted.

Thrump 3♠

Picture the following. You hold:

♠ Q853   ♡ A872   ◊ AK4   ♣ J3

Partner opens 1◊, but before you can begin your search for a major-suit fit, your RHO jumps to 3♣. No problem, you say, with your perfect negative double.

Unfortunately, partner answers by bidding 3◊. Now what? You could support diamonds, but 5◊ is nobody's favorite contract. If partner has a hand like:

♠ K9   ♡ Q63   ◊ Q97542   ♣ KQ   or

♠ A72   ♡ J4   ◊ QJ10932   ♣ A4

3NT is ice cold, but I do not like our chances in 5◊.

Here is my solution. After opener's very disappointing 3◊ rebid, responder can follow up by bidding 3♠ (artificial, as well as alertable). Instead of showing a modest hand with long spades, **3♠ would be begging opener to bid 3NT with a club stopper**. That seems far more to the point.

When exactly would this "thrump 3♠" bid be made? Any time the auction proceeds as follows: partner opens at the one level (in any suit but spades) and the overcall is specifically 3♣. These are the only applicable auctions.

West	North	East	South
1 suit (not spades)	3♣	Dbl	Pass
3◊ or 3♡	Pass	**3♠**	

Enemy preempts can make our life difficult, but we can get revenge with special conventions like this.

Low-Level Negative Doubles
with No Unbid Major

Here is another Bergen brainchild. Do not blame it on anyone else. This concept applies to three auctions:

1♡ - (1♠) - Dbl   1♠ - (2♡) - Dbl   1♡ - (2♠) - Dbl

Negative doubles were invented to allow responder to show his unbid major(s). On these auctions, there is none. What remains is showing the unbid minors, which is not very important. In fact, it is impossible to indicate both. For instance, after the auction begins 1♠ - (2♡) - ?, responder must double with:

♠ A7 ♡ 43 ◇ J98653 ♣ A74

He needs to take some action with this hand, but is not strong enough for a forcing bid of 3◇.

When there are no unbid majors, the main purpose of a negative double is to show some values with a hand that lacks a good, natural bid. Describing responder's overall strength is more important than promising a specific minor suit.

Therefore, I limit responder's range for a negative double on these three auctions to less than an opening bid. After a 1♠ overcall, the double shows 6-11 HCP while the range for the 2♡ and 2♠ overcalls is 9-11.

Worth noting: after the two-level overcalls, responder's bid of a new minor at the three level is natural and forcing to game. This part of the treatment represents standard practice.

Therefore, after 1♡ - (1♠) - ?

♠ 873 ♡ A10 ◇ KJ65 ♣ AQ43
(Bid 2♣. It is usually right to bid up the line with four-card suits. A negative double would have denied an opening bid.)

♠ 54 ♡ K7 ◇ A9543 ♣ AQ64
(Bid 2◇.)

Similarly, after 1♠ - (2♡) - ?

♠ 5 ♡ Q6 ◇ AKQ4 ♣ QJ7653
(Bid 3♣.)

♠ K8 ♡ 763 ◇ AKQ8 ♣ J984
(Bid 3◇, not 3♣, because the diamonds are much stronger.)

♠ A ♡ 76 ◇ AJ8653 ♣ 10643
(Double. Your hand is not strong enough for a 3◇ bid.)

After 1♡ - (2♠) - ?

♠ 7542 ♡ Q ◇ AQ104 ♣ AQ74
(Bid 3♣, forcing to game.)

♠ A ♡ A7 ◇ KQ754 ♣ 108763
(Bid 3◇. Always bid the higher suit first with 5-5.)

♠ 98 ♡ 8 ◇ AKJ6 ♣ Q87543
(Double.)

Is this treatment worth playing? I like it, but as always the choice is yours.

Partnership Checklists

Bread and Butter Issues

Indicate the agreement for your partnership on each of the following topics. The Bergen suggestion is on the right.

Negative doubles: how high?   5 ♦

After 1♣ - (1♦), can responder bid a four-card major?   Yes

After 1 minor - (1♡), does 1♠ promise five spades?   Yes

Does a negative double guarantee both unbid suits?

1♣ - (1♦) - Dbl	Yes
1♦ - (1♠) - Dbl	No
1♡ - (1♠) - Dbl	No
1♦ - (2♣) - Dbl	No

Thrump doubles of jump overcalls (3♦ through 3♠):

Do we play them?	Yes
Do they deny a stopper in overcaller's suit?	Yes
Do they promise the unbid major(s)?	No

Is responder's jump shift weak after a simple overcall?   Yes

Is 4NT unusual by responder after a 4♡ or 4♠ overcall?   Yes

Opener's Bread and Butter Issues

After responder makes a negative double:

Can opener introduce a three-card minor?	Yes
Can opener introduce a three-card major?	Yes
Can opener rebid a five-card minor?	Yes
Can opener rebid a five-card major?	Yes
Does a 1NT rebid guarantee a stopper in the enemy's suit?	No
Does a double jump to 3NT promise an unbalanced hand?	Yes
Is opener's jump shift forcing to game?	No
Is 4NT unusual by opener after a 4♡ or 4♠ overcall?	Yes

Advanced Issues

Indicate the agreement for your partnership on each of these topics. Warning: do not add too much to your repertoire at once.

Can responder be 4-3 in the majors on the following auction:

1♣ - (1♢) - Dbl?

When responder has made a negative double that shows a four-card major, can he have three very good ones instead?

Can responder raise opener's minor with good three-card support?

After 1 of a minor - (1♡), can responder bid 1♠ with:

A strong four-card suit?
A weak four-card suit?

On the following auctions, 1♡ - (1♠), 1♠ - (2♡) and 1♡ - (2♠), does a negative double deny an opening bid?

Can responder "preempt a preempt" after 1 suit - (jump overcall)?

Do we play "thrump 3♠"?

Is responder's jump cuebid a transfer to 3NT?

Bridge Jargon

4NT Unusual—After an opponent overcalls four of a major, if the next bid by opener or responder is 4NT, it is not Blackwood. The bid asks partner to bid a suit at the five level.

Michaels Cuebid—An overcall in the opponent's suit that shows at least 5-5 in two other suits, with emphasis on the unbid major(s).

Penalty Pass—A pass of partner's negative or takeout double, hoping to score up a substantial penalty. At low levels, only made with length and strength in the opponent's suit.

Responder's Jump Cuebid as a Notrump Transfer—A Bergen convention designed to place the opponents at a disadvantage when leading the suit they overcalled.

Thrump 3♠—An artificial followup to a three-level negative double where responder is trying hard to get to 3NT.

Thrump Double—An important Bergen convention after a 3-level WJO. Responder hopes that opener has a stopper and can bid 3NT. Double does not promise length in the unbid major(s).

Trap Pass—A pass by a player based on an imposing holding in the opponent's suit. The trap passer is hoping for the opportunity to make a subsequent penalty pass if partner reopens with a double.

Weak Jump Overcalls (WJO)—After RHO opens, a jump shows a weak hand with a long, strong suit. Similar to a weak two-bid.

Weak Jump Shifts (WJS) in Competition— A jump by responder in an unbid suit is preemptive after an overcall or double.

Learning With Marty

Hardcover Books by Marty Bergen

More Declarer Play the Bergen Way How to Make More Contracts	$18.95
Declarer Play the Bergen Way 2005 Bridge Book of the year!	$18.95
Bergen for the Defense Sharpen Your Defensive Skills	$18.95
MARTY SEZ... Volume 1 Bergen's Bevy of Bridge Secrets	$17.95
MARTY SEZ... Volume 2 More Secrets of Winning Bridge	$17.95
MARTY SEZ... Volume 3 Practical Tips You Can Take to the Bank	$17.95
POINTS SCHMOINTS! All-time Bestseller and Bridge Book of the Year	$19.95
More POINTS SCHMOINTS! Sequel to the Award-Winning Bestseller	$19.95

•• VERY SPECIAL OFFER ••

Buy one of these hardcover books from Marty
and receive a **free** autographed copy of any one
of his seven most recent softcover books.
Buy 2 hardcovers and get 3 free softcover books etc!
Personalized books available upon request.

Softcover Books by Marty Bergen
Buy 2, then get 1 (equal or lesser price) for half price

Bergen's Best Bridge Tips	$7.95
Bergen's Best Bridge Quizzes, Vol. 1	$7.95
To Open or Not to Open	$6.95
Better Rebidding with Bergen	$7.95
Understanding 1NT Forcing	$5.95
Hand Evaluation: Points, Schmoints!	$7.95
Introduction to Negative Doubles	$7.95
Negative Doubles	$10.95

Interactive CDs
• • **FREE SHIPPING** (in the U.S.) if you mention this book • •

by Marty Bergen

POINTS SCHMOINTS!	~~$29.95~~	$25
Marty Sez...	~~$24.95~~	$20

Very Special Offer: Get both Bergen CDs for $30!
For free demos, e-mail Marty at: mbergen@mindspring.com

4 CDs by Larry Cohen
Free demos available at: http://www.larryco.com/index.html

~~$29.95 each~~   **$19 each**!

2 **CDs by Kit Woolsey**   ~~$29.95 each~~   **$19 each**!

Software By Fred Gitelman
"Best software ever created for improving your declarer play."
Bridge Master 2000   ~~$59.95~~ $48

**Mention this book and receive a free Bergen softcover (choice of 7) with each Gitelman CD.

♠ ♡ # Bridge Cruises ◇ ♣
with Marty Bergen and Larry Cohen

For prices, itinerary, flyers, etc. or to be on the mailing list for Marty and Larry cruises, call Bruce Travel at 1-800-367-9980. To participate in bridge activities, you must book the cruise with Bruce Travel. These cruises feature daily lessons, as much duplicate bridge as you care to play (withACBL masterpoints), plus all the activities, entertainment and ambiance that you'd would expect to find on a first-class cruise ship.

All Bergen cruises feature:
Brand-new material
Free Bergen book for all who sign up early.
Free drawing to play duplicate on cruise with Marty.
Free private lesson for groups of 5+ who sign up together.

ORDERING INFORMATION
To place your order, call Marty toll-free at:
1-800-386-7432

All major credit cards are welcome

Or send a check or money order (U.S. funds), to:
Marty Bergen
9 River Chase Terrace
Palm Beach Gardens, FL 33418-6817

If ordering by mail, please call or email for S&H details